Simple and Usable

web, mobile, and interaction design

Giles Colborne

New Riders | VOICES THAT MATTER™

Simple and Usable Web, Mobile, and Interaction Design
Giles Colborne

New Riders
1249 Eighth Street
Berkeley, CA 94710
510/524-2178
510/524-2221 (fax)

Find us on the Web at: www.newriders.com
To report errors, please send a note to errata@peachpit.com

New Riders is an imprint of Peachpit, a division of Pearson Education.

Project Editor: Michael J. Nolan
Development Editor: Margaret Anderson/Stellarvisions
Production Editor: Becky Winter
Copyeditor: Gretchen Dykstra
Proofreader: Gretchen Dykstra
Indexer: Joy Dean Lee
Book Designer: Mimi Heft

ISBN 13: 978-0-321-70354-5
ISBN 10:   0-321-70354-5

9 8 7 6 5 4 3

Printed and bound in the United States of America

For my wife and children, Pey, Leah and Bea

Thanks

Writing this book was anything but simple, an irony that has not been lost on me. Many people have worked long, hard hours to bring it to life.

Firstly, I have to thank my family, Pey, Leah, Bea and my parents, for putting up with me while I was writing it, for the ideas they gave me, and for making room for this in our lives.

The team at Peachpit have been fantastic. Thanks to the book's editor Margaret Anderson, who gave sage advice and vital encouragement throughout; Michael Nolan who took on this project, editor-in-chief Nancy Davis; Gretchen Dykstra for her eagle eye and can-do enthusiasm; Mimi Heft for her lovely design; Becky Winter and Danielle Foster for such hard work on production and Glenn Bisignani for bringing it to people's attention.

My colleagues at cxpartners made a huge contribution to the writing of this book, in particular in patiently bashing the ideas into shape: Richard Caddick, Joe Leech, Verity Whitmore, Anna Thompson, Danielle Gould, Chui Tan, Walt Buchan, Neil Schwarz, Anthony Mace, Jesmond Allen, Fiz Yazdi, James Rosenberg, and Nik Lazell— great people to work with.

Advice and support from other authors was invaluable as I stepped outside my comfort zone. Thank you Steve Krug, Kevlin Henney, Yang-May Ooi, Jason Cranford Teague, Louis Rosenfeld, Caroline Jarrett, and Whitney Quesenbery.

Thanks to all those people who helped me with inspirational interviews Naomi Pearce, Ken Case of Omni Group, Rich Siegel of Bare Bones Software, Jürgen Schweizer, Keith Lang, Barney Kirby, Mariana Cavalcanti, Bill Schallenberg, Luis Babicek, Ken Kellogg, Fran Dattilo, and all the folks at Marriott, Alan Colville, David Jarvis, and Pete Greenwood.

Thanks also to the people who gave me feedback and ideas throughout: Tyler Tate, Bonny Colville-Hyde, Dot Pinkney, Jon Tan, Donna Spencer, Dave Ellender, Ian Fenn, Matthew Keeler and the folks at the University of Bath and Bristol Usability Group, Brenda Bazylewski, and the dozens of other people who've contributed, helped, and inspired me.

Contents

Part 3

Four strategies for simplicity

Part 4

Remove

Part 5
Organize

Part 6
Hide

Part 7

Displace

Part 8

Before we go

Part 1

Why are we here?

A story about simplicity

The first printer I bought was a fussy device. Setting it up involved fitting together several parts and going on an extra trip into town because the correct cable wasn't included. When I returned, I had to read my computer's manual to check some hardware settings, open up the printer case, and use a paperclip to set some switches to match. After a few tries I got it right. Then I had to install driver software onto the computer. The whole process took hours of mistakes, cursing, and painstaking work.

The same could be said of any number of encounters with technology over the years: setting up a mobile phone, plugging a laptop into a plasma display, or reading a webpage that takes three screens and 113 links to tell me the weather. Technology that is supposed to make our lives easier often feels like it's on the march against us.

This year I bought a new printer for my home. The setup process was: take it out of the box, remove the orange sticky tape that was holding the delicate parts in place, pop in the cartridge, and switch it on. At which point the printer informed me that it would like to join my WiFi network and could it have a password, please? And that was it. The printer and my computer got along just fine. Setting up a new printer seemed as simple as plugging in a new radio.

It left me thinking: why can't it always be like this?

It's not the first time I've asked that question. I've spent my career trying to make technology simple. The problem is that a lot of advice on simplicity is rather vague: "less is more" and all that. So I've tried to find some strategies that seem to work, and real examples and stories to share.

Why should setting up a printer be any harder than plugging it in?

The power of simplicity

In 2007, Jonathan Kaplan and Ariel Braunstein turned the US camcorder market on its head by creating a camcorder that was simpler than anything else on the market.

At the time, companies like Sony and Panasonic were trying to win sales by adding advanced features such as the ability to add Hollywood-style captions and video effects in the camera.

By comparison, the Flip was crude, with low resolution and missing "basic" features like optical zoom. One year later the Flip had come from nowhere to sell a million units—at a time when the entire US market was just 6 million units.

Kaplan and Braunstein realized that camcorders had become complex and intimidating. Most people didn't want to produce feature films at home—they wanted to pull out a camera, capture a spontaneous event, and share it on YouTube.

The Flip concentrated on making that as simple as possible, ditching any features that were not essential. There were no cables that could get lost or left behind, just a flip-out USB connector that gave the camera its name. There were only nine buttons, including a big red record button. There wasn't even a CD of software for your computer—the necessary software was stored on the camcorder itself and you could download it when you first connected the Flip to your Mac or PC.

Simple products, like the Flip, the original VW Beetle, and Twitter, often have a profound effect on markets. They are easy to use, so they find a popular audience; they are reliable, so people develop an attachment to them; and they are adaptable, so they end up being used in surprising ways.

Thanks to the web, mobile phones, and low-cost computers, the audience for technology is becoming ever wider. There is a growing opportunity for releasing products that are simple yet powerful.

People love simple, dependable, adaptable products.

Increasing complexity
is unsustainable

Complex products are fascinating. Back in 2006, technology columnist David Pogue dubbed this the "Sport Utility Principle: People like to surround themselves with unnecessary power."

It's not a bad analogy. At the time, the US motor industry was based on building and selling cars that were big, heavy, expensive, thirsty, and sold at a premium. The motor companies quickly became reliant on selling extras. Then came the economic crash of 2008. Suddenly, no one wanted that unnecessary power. The motor companies found they had driven down a blind alley and that it was going to take years and billions of dollars to put things right.

Continually adding features to software turns out to be equally unsustainable.

The more features you add, the less chance you have of coming across a new feature that is of real value to someone. Sooner or later, your new features are going to fall flat. Adding complexity also means you're building a massive legacy of code that makes your product more expensive to maintain, which also makes it hard to react to changes in the market.

Meanwhile, your users become increasingly dissatisfied with your product. The added complexity means they can't easily find the features that are important to them. They also start to resent the fact that they're paying for features they don't use.

Like the car giants in 2008, you may find that users' appetite for more quickly turns against you.

All that unnecessary
power comes
at a price.

Not that kind of simple

I was once called in to review a company's new business intranet. It had recently been redesigned, but the salespeople complained that it was making their work impossibly complex.

The salespeople showed me how they had to fill in page after page of forms every time they met a potential client. I was puzzled why such a bureaucratic system had been put in place.

Then I talked to the managers who had set up the intranet. They told me how wonderful the new intranet was and how much time and effort it was saving them because it "automatically" generated the reports they needed.

Sure enough, the reports exactly matched the forms the salespeople now had to complete. The managers had made their lives considerably simpler—by making the salespeople's lives more complicated.

When you're designing any piece of technology, there are at least three perspectives: the manager's, the engineer's, and the user's.

This book is about the user's perspective: it's about making things *feel* simple to use.

Sometimes you can create simple user experiences with simple technology, or simple management, but that's not a certainty. Google deploys complex technology and employs thousands of people to make it easy to find information on the Internet.

What feels simple to one person in one situation may not feel simple to everyone in every situation. A Formula One driver won't feel his life has been made simpler if you ask him to race in a Mini. But while it's a fun puzzle to design complex systems for experienced users, technology becomes interesting when it gets out of the hands of experts and finds a wider audience.

This book is concerned primarily with the experience of mainstream users.

Simpler than a bike.
Until you try to ride it.

Character

Simple doesn't mean minimal. Stripped-down designs can still have their own character and personality.

Take two simple chairs: a Shaker chair and a Panton chair. Each reduces the chair to its basic components. Each is easy to manufacture, given the technology available at the time it was designed. And each solves a different problem: the Shaker chair is hard-wearing, the Panton chair is stackable.

The two designs are simple and basic, yet they have utterly distinctive characters and uses.

The materials you use, the emphasis you place on the key elements, and the way you combine even a few elements will have a dramatic effect on the final design. People will recognize and put value on the small differences, just as they focus on the small differences between Google and Bing searches or between one online bank and another.

> Simplicity does not mean want or poverty. It does not mean the absence of any decor, or absolute nudity. It only means that the decor should belong intimately to the design proper, and that anything foreign to it should be taken away.
>
> —*Paul Jacques Grillo (Form, Function and Design)*

In other words, you can be simple without being minimalist. The character and personality should come from the medium you're using, the brand you're representing, and the task that users are undertaking.

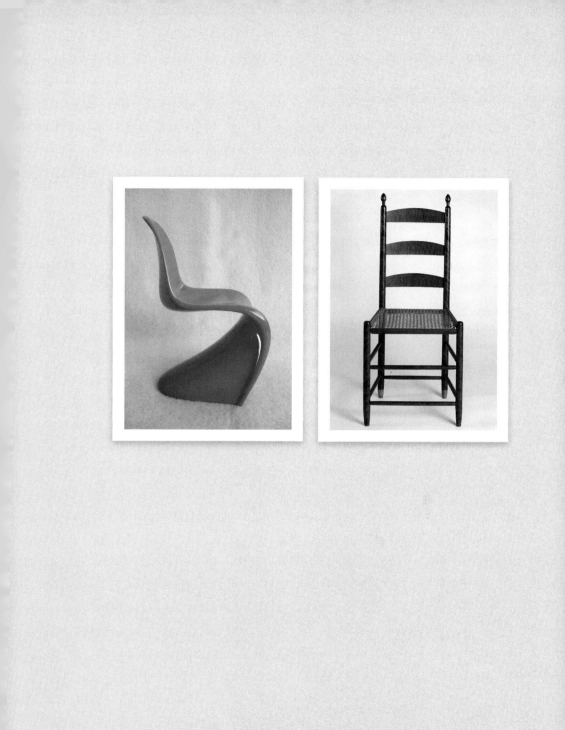

Both simple. But each has a unique character.

Fake simplicity

When something is simple, it looks effortless. So it is always disheartening to discover how hard it is to achieve simplicity. Surely there must be an easier way to reach the goal?

You'll find people pushing ideas to deliver fake simplicity. Like diet pills, laser sights for golf clubs, and "get rich while working from home" schemes, fake simplicity never lives up to the initial promise. Instead, it ends up making things more complex and less effective.

But, remarkably, some fake simplicity has become received wisdom. It's a collection of techniques that are quick, relatively cheap, and uncontroversial.

Because of that, you'll find that whenever things get hard, these ideas crop up.

And because everyone "knows" these things work, no one ever gets blamed when they fail.

Instead, people use fake simplicity to say "I'm trying" to the world without ever having to try very hard or be very good.

Instructions seem to say, "See how much effort we've made to explain this to you? If you don't get it, it's your own fault." So they're a great way of faking it, because they shift responsibility for failure onto the user. The problem is that most people don't bother reading instructions: they prefer to get on with doing.

Wizards promise to make things simple by breaking them down into steps. The problem is they take control away from the user. Because of this, wizards feel constricting. It may be possible to herd users through a brief wizard, but the longer it goes on, the worse it feels.

Creating magic characters who can predict the users' needs and tell them what to do is another example of fake simplicity. The theory is that hearing instructions from a character is friendly and human. But computers can't accurately predict your needs or tell if you're becoming annoyed with them. Seeing a message in a suggestion box on-screen is one thing. Being told what to do by a cartoon character is another.

Sticking these kinds of extras on rarely makes an experience feel simple.

Simplicity isn't something you can stick on top of a user interface.

Know yourself

It can seem as though organizations have an immune response to making things simple.

A few years ago, I spoke to a manager at an automotive company who'd been tasked with simplifying their product range. Every time he tried to cut an option, he'd get a complaint from one of the salespeople: that option is vital to one of my customers. Even if the customer provided a tiny percentage of the company's entire business, the salesperson would point out: well, they're *my* most important client.

Sorting out that conflict requires someone more senior to step in. In which case you need to make your case in terms the management can accept. Companies tend to measure success by making money and growing. So before you try to simplify a user experience, you must understand how the company behind it works. Here's a trick from Peter Merholz of Adaptive Path:

Most companies are driven by an equation. Something like:

(number of cars sold) x (price of car) - (cost of overhead) = (profit)

You need to understand how simplifying the user experience could affect each of those elements. Will making the products simpler enable the company to sell more cars (for instance, because they'll be more desirable) or at a higher price (because they'll be seen as more sophisticated) or at a lower overhead (because the components will be less expensive)?

Next, you need to prioritize those changes. A good way to do this is to plot out how important each change is versus how feasible it is. If you ask people, they'll tell you that everything is important and anything is feasible. Instead, get them to divide up a fixed number of points (or Monopoly money or jelly beans) for importance and a fixed number of points for feasibility.

The changes that sit at the top right-hand corner of your graph are your priorities, and they are what your improvements need to address. If you can show you're doing that, you'll be able to make a case for simplifying.

The next step is to set a vision for what a simple user experience might be.

Leave these

Consider these

Do these

5

Importance

- Increase profit margin

- Improve demand

- Reduce cost of components

- Decrease customer returns
- Decrease defects during manufacture

- Reduce sale price

0   Practicality   5

Part 2

Setting a vision

Two ways to describe what's core

Whether you're designing an entire website or a drop-down menu, you need a vision of what a simple experience should be. A vision gives you a way of judging whether you're keeping things simple.

I have two ways of doing this.

The quick and dirty way is to write down a one-line description, in the simplest terms possible, of what I'm creating, along with a few guidelines I want to stick to. So when I find myself tied in knots over designing a comparison table, I take a step back and ask myself, "What is this for?" That description becomes my benchmark for a simple design. This usually works well when I am designing something very small (like one page in a larger website) and when I know more or less what I have to design.

The better and longer way is to describe the experience I want the users to have. That means describing the users' world and how my design fits in. This works well when I am designing something big (like an entire website or a mobile device) because it makes me think through the problem in more detail.

Describing the users' experience is also helpful when I'm not sure what the answer to the design problem is. By the time I've set down the goals and constraints, I can see what solutions will not work and I've usually had enough time to think of a few ideas that will.

This approach is good when I need to get agreement from other people because I can talk them through the constraints I've had to consider and then show how my solution fits.

In other words, the long route to understanding the users' world, their preferences, and their behavior is almost always the one required, so I'll explain that first.

Every design is a solution that has to sit within constraints. The best way to begin is by understanding those constraints. Then you can ensure your design fits into the spaces in people's lives.

**First, understand
the users' world,
then figure out how
your design fits in.**

Get out of your office

Begin by visiting the place where people will use your software. Most designs are reviewed in quiet meeting rooms where everyone gives the design their full attention. People rarely use software in such a calm setting. Simple user experiences need to work in disruptive, changing environments.

A few years ago I was asked to redesign some software to help car dealers put together a marketing plan. The brief was to merge several components into one, so that a dealer could write a plan in one sitting.

Fortunately, a colleague of mine visited some dealerships to talk to the managers about their needs. At the first dealership she visited, the manager sat in an office with a glass front that opened onto the showroom. As they spoke, the manager kept glancing up to scan the showroom. Whenever a customer looked lost, he would hurry out and attend to them. It was the same in every dealership she visited: the managers were constantly interrupted by the needs of their customers.

Instead of merging the components, we needed to break them into smaller chunks so that the managers could complete them in the short bursts of time they had.

Visiting users in their workplaces was vital—if we'd simply imagined the manager at his desk we would have missed the crucial aspects.

Watching people in the real world is quick and you rarely need to pay anyone to do it. Even with minimal planning you can learn a lot.

If you can't get permission to do it, then talk to some users about where they are and what's happening when they use your software.

I was recently asked to review a mobile website that had been pro-moted during a rugby tournament. The owners couldn't understand why users dropped out of the site after a couple of minutes—their exit points didn't correspond to any obvious usability problems.

When I interviewed users, the answer became clear: they had been using the site during the ad breaks. When the rugby came back on, they went back to watching TV. The site took too long to get through.

You can't control the environments where people use your software. You have to design it to fit.

The best place to watch users is in their natural environment.

What to look for

When you get into the real world you'll notice lots of ways that people's experience can be affected. Here are some things to be ready for.

Offices

- In open-plan offices, staff frequently distract each other—watch and you'll be surprised how often people are interrupted or drop what they're doing because they've overheard something interesting.

- Telephones, instant messaging, and email interrupt users constantly.

- When people print documents for a meeting, they tend to wait until the last minute. Things go wrong when they're flustered.

Homes

- People use their laptops while watching television or listening to the radio, with their attention and time divided unpredictably between the two.

- Home broadband connections may not be as reliable or as fast as office lines, especially at peak times in the evening.

- Mothers grocery shopping online while the children watch a cartoon have to select around 100 items from a possible 30,000 in about 30 minutes.

Outdoors

- Stand on a busy street corner and you'll see people checking directions on their phones as they walk up to the intersection. If they have to spend time puzzling over instructions, it could be fatal.

- People may be carrying bags while they try to use their mobile phones, making it harder for them to tap on small buttons.

- People check mobile apps in queues everywhere—they may be interrupted at any time.

- Bright sunlight can make it hard to read mobile screens outdoors.

- Larger devices, such as tablets, quickly start to feel heavy and uncomfortable, making people want to put them down.

Your user experience needs to be simple enough to work among the distractions and fit into the cracks between interruptions.

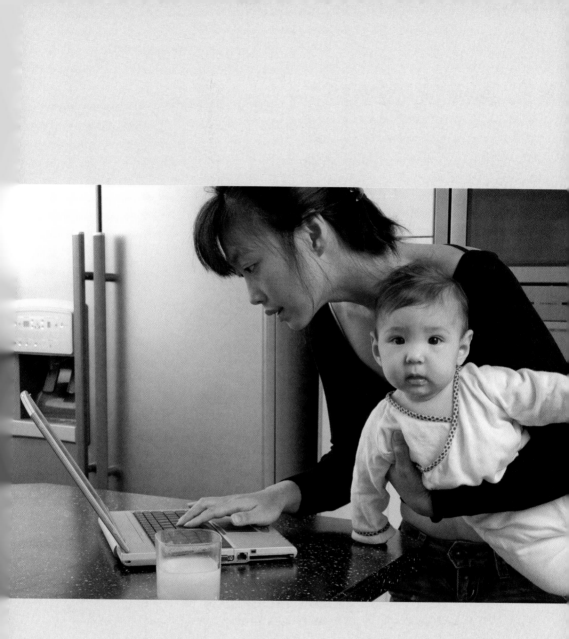

At home, at work, and outdoors, you must design for constant interruptions.

Three types of user

When it comes to simplicity, you can divide users into three types.

Experts are happy to explore your product or service and to push the limits of what it can do. They want never-before-seen technology that is customized for them. Even if they're new to a product, they have an expert attitude. In other words, they'll spend time finding out how it works and exploring new features. If you're making a mobile phone, these are the people who want to be able to browse through the mobile phone's file system and tweak everything. It turns out there are relatively few people like this.

I call the next group **willing adopters**. They probably already use some similar products or services. They're tempted to use something more sophisticated, but they're not comfortable playing with something entirely new—they need to be given easy ways to adopt new features. For instance, they might be interested in a more sophisticated phone, but only if they can transfer their precious contacts easily. There are fewer of these people than you'd imagine and their tolerance for learning is pretty low.

The vast majority of people are **mainstreamers**. They don't use technology for its own sake; they use it to get a job done. They tend to learn a few key features and never add to their repertoire. These are the people who say, "I just want my mobile phone to work." Most people fall into this group.

It's tempting to think that after a while, people graduate from one group to another. But that hardly ever happens. Even after years of using a product, people tend to stay in the same group.

For example, take any large group of people who've been using Microsoft Excel for five years. You'll find some people who've explored settings and options, some who've got a few specialist features set up to do what they like, and others who just use it for adding up columns of figures.

It has more to do with their underlying attitude toward technology than the amount of time they spend using a product or service.

It's tempting to design for the first two groups—they're easier to please. But experiences that feel simple are designed for the mainstreamers.

The vast majority of users are mainstreamers; experts and willing adopters are a minority. For example, in 2009, complex cameras like SLRs comprised only 9 percent of the digital camera market (source: CIPA).

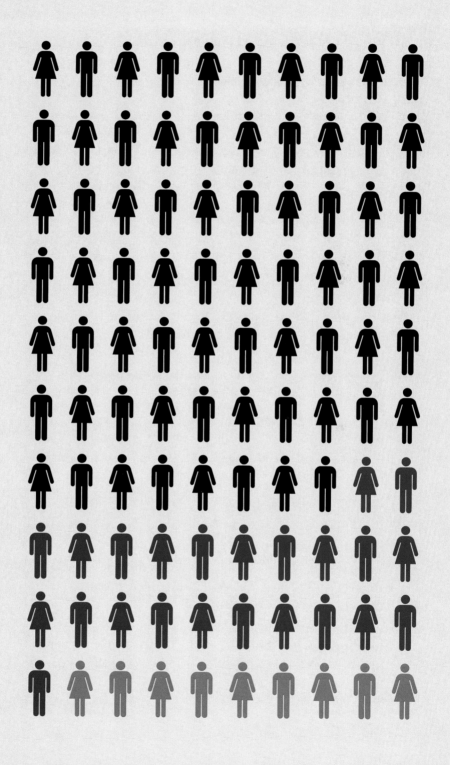

Why you should ignore expert customers

Most companies spend too much time listening to their expert customers—the ones who spend the most time using their products or services—because they're easy to talk to. Expert customers are enthusiasts, they're vocal and opinionated about how to improve what's on offer.

But experts aren't typical customers and their judgment is often skewed. They don't experience the problems that mainstream customers have.

And they want things that mainstream customers don't care about.

Here's what one responder on Slashdot (a blog run by experts and enthusiasts) had to say when the iPod was announced: "No wireless. Less space than a Nomad. Lame."

Another commenter wrote: "I don't see many sales in the future of iPod." And another: "All I can say is, as an Apple 'fan', I'm sad."

Commenters on another enthusiast blog, MacRumors, also wanted more: "I still can't believe this! All this hype for something so ridiculous! Who cares about an MP3 player?"

Apple's expert customers wanted a flying car. Apple's mainstream customers just wanted an MP3 player that worked.

I see this again and again: a small group of customers make noisy, persistent demands for new features that are too complicated for typical users.

You'll find it hard to convince your stakeholders (who are insiders, and therefore experts) that the customers who are also experts (just like them) are not the ones you should listen to. After all, your best customers spend a lot of time and money per head; they're so easy to talk to—they come to you, they get what you do, and they speak your language; and they're so reasonable—if you ask them to upgrade to the latest version, they do it without hesitating.

But if you listen to them first, you'll create products that are too complex for mainstream customers to use.

As of January 2010, Apple had sold 240,000,000 iPods and no flying cars.

So if your stakeholders are trying to create a mass-market product by listening to their expert customers, remind them of this story. Sometimes, it's best to ignore your expert customers.

Experts often want features that would horrify mainstreamers.

Design for the mainstream

The middle ground looks safer. Unlike the demanding enthusiasts, the willing adopters would like to use some fancy new features, as long as you make them just a bit easier.

Most "usable" design tends to focus on this group. People who already book their flights online are invited to user tests for travel websites. People who already use the camera on their mobile phone are asked to test camera phones. So we design for people who aren't very hard to please.

You can learn a lot by watching these people. Every user test I've watched revealed some way to improve a website or a mobile phone. But by focusing on these people, we're making it easy on ourselves.

These users will put up with the problems they've grown used to (like needing to dig around on their mobile phone to find their photos) because they've learned to tolerate them.

But these willing adopters are still not typical. They're a small, extreme group who have more skills and more perseverance than mainstream users. It's just that they're a bit less extreme than the experts.

If you want simplicity, if you want to be seen as an innovator, then it's the mainstream customers you should be aiming at. The Ford Model T wasn't the first car ever built, but it was the first one made with the mass market in mind. Henry Ford revolutionized the motor industry because he aimed squarely at the typical person. Simplicity was at the heart of his vision:

> We will build a motor car for the great multitude. It will be…small enough for the individual to run and care for. It will be constructed…after the simplest designs modern engineering can devise. But it will be so low in price that no man making a good salary will be unable to own one.
>
> — *Henry Ford, on the Model T*

All of Ford's innovations (his use of production lines, the price point of his car, the easy-to-maintain engine design) came as a result of his desire to focus on creating a simple product that was suitable for the mainstream.

If you want to make something simple, design for the multitude.

If designing for experts is like building a car for mechanics, then designing for the middle ground is like building one for people who like tinkering with engines. The typical user is a mainstreamer.

Mass appeal comes from focusing on the mainstream.

What mainstreamers want

When you're setting your vision, make sure the mainstreamer is at the heart of it so you can't sneak in the convenient skills of the expert to get you out of a tricky design problem.

- Mainstreamers are interested in getting the job done now; experts are interested in customizing their settings first.

- Mainstreamers value ease of control; experts value precision of control.

- Mainstreamers want reliable results; experts want perfect results.

- Mainstreamers are afraid of breaking something; experts want to take things apart to see how they work.

- Mainstreamers want a good match; experts want an exact match.

- Mainstreamers want examples and stories; experts want principles.

Don't assume you can teach users much or that instructions will help them. When they're under pressure, mainstreamers tend to forget what they've learned, ignore instructions, and revert to behaving like novices.

You've probably experienced that for yourself: when you've got a deadline or when you're distracted, that's when you delete your vital file or the printer starts spewing out the wrong document.

Simple user experiences need to work for a novice, or a mainstreamer who's under pressure.

Mainstreamers don't want to build it from scratch.

Emotional needs

Jürgen Schweizer is one of the developers of Things, an award-winning iPhone "to-do list" app. He points out that understanding what your design should do is often trivial: "At first glance, a to-do list is just a list of items with a checkbox next to each one so the user can see what's been completed."

However, people are driven by an emotional need. Even with something as straightforward as a to-do list, they want to use the app for a reason.

Understanding the emotional goal helps you see what's really important in your design, says Jürgen:

> When we thought about why people would use our software, we realized that they had a lot on their plate. They wanted to achieve a lot and still feel in control. They needed to be able to capture a thousand items and yet not feel overwhelmed when they looked at the list. So we put a lot of effort into making sure that they'd only ever look at a handful of the most important things, but they'd be able to find all their other notes and reminders just when they needed them.

Of course anyone making a quick note of a to-do item won't think about that at the time, so their lists can easily get out of control. What starts off feeling simple can end up feeling complex. But Jürgen didn't want the app to annoy users by interrupting them as they were making notes with demands that they organize them.

That insight led the Things team to spend time finding natural and helpful ways to organize and filter tasks. As Jürgen points out, getting that right turned out to be a very subtle and complex problem. "It turned out to be about making the user feel good about putting things off. We needed to make the user feel confident that they'd be able to put tasks away and find them again later." Solving that problem is what made Things stand out from hundreds of other iPhone task managers to become such a popular app.

The time spent discussing those deeper, emotional needs helped the developers of Things understand the real reason people needed their software, and so made them focus on an important set of hidden needs.

A getting things done app needs to be more than just a notepad. It needs to help users feel organized and relaxed. The Things app does this because it has a simple, flexible way of categorizing users' to-do items.

Even a to-do list has to satisfy emotional needs.

Simplicity is about control

Unraveling your users' emotional needs can be tricky, and made worse by the fact that many people are uncomfortable sitting in a design meeting talking about feelings.

Fortunately, when it comes to designing for simplicity, the key emotional need is for users to feel that they're in control.

Firstly, they want to feel in control of the technology they're using.

Experts want to control and customize the technology. You'll need to take the mainstreamers' view of "control:" to be in control of the outcomes. They don't want to worry about the software or technology, and they don't want it to tell them what to do. Mainstreamers want control that is easy, reliable, and quick.

Your design shouldn't interfere with this sense of control. It should extend it. Simple experiences make users confident that they're making good choices. Simple experiences reassure users that the product will respond in a predictable way.

Secondly, they want to feel in control of their lives.

Sometimes being in control is about completing a task: a woman buying a dress wants to feel in control of how she looks. Sometimes it's about getting information: a man reading the news wants to understand what's happening in his world (in order to feel in control).

Begin with that need—the user's need to feel in control of some part of his life—then try to dig deeper by asking, "So what?"

Take the example of the Things app from the previous section. The users' overall need is to be in control. So what? For a task manager, they need to capture lots of tasks. So what? Having too many tasks on their to-do list means they'll feel overwhelmed. So what? They need to be able to limit what they see to what's relevant at any one time. So what? We need to come up with an easy, way to organize their lists.

Repeatedly asking "so what" eventually throws up an emotional need, a rational need, and a solution. It also helps you arrive at a deeper understanding of the design problem you want to solve. (Of course, you'll need to check your thinking by talking to real users).

Once you understand who your users are and what drives them, you'll have some of your most important insights.

Simplicity is about feeling in control.

Choosing the right "what"

The next question is, "What is the user doing?"

Often things are complex because a design ignores important steps. For instance, most video cameras seem to concentrate on taking movies. But once you've taken video, you want to share it quickly, something that's rather tricky for most video cameras.

One of the reasons the Flip camcorder feels so convenient is because it does both things equally well.

The thing to do, then, is to describe what the user does from the beginning to the end of their experience, remembering that it's the user's actions you're most interested in, not the thing you're designing. If you describe your solution in too much detail at this stage, you may end up painting yourself into a corner. Instead, just go to a level of detail that's sufficient to complete the picture. You might start with "Take and share movies," to begin with, then list each step the user will take, keeping a consistent level of detail.

The point is to see every step of the user's experience.

Make sure you describe what's happening in the user's language or you risk losing track of what's core. People who use Facebook aren't "social networking," they're sharing pictures and news with friends. If you get away from describing things as the user sees them, you'll end up writing a story about a database or a mobile phone instead of about the user.

Focus on the main action and describe it as the user sees it.

**Make sure you
don't miss any
important steps.**

Describing the user experience

Once you've researched your problem, you need to turn it into a vision. A story is a great way to describe your vision. Unlike a list of requirements, it helps the reader understand what's important and why.

In case you're worried that stories aren't very businesslike or technical: don't be. Managers use stories all the time (mission statements, for instance) and technical teams tell stories (flowcharts and use cases). User experience teams have been writing stories for a long time, too.

A story should sum up the core experience in a few sentences. For a video camera like the Flip, it could be:

> You're on a city street when you hear a commotion: Paris Hilton is walking toward you. You pull your Flip camera out of your pocket and hand it to a stranger, asking her to video you with Paris in the background. Then you hurry to a nearby friend's house where you use her computer to share your movie online, without any instructions.

If you're trying to design a video camera, this story tells you what's important:

- It's a camera that's small enough to carry anywhere; it's the kind of thing you'll have on you when you go out, rather than a bulky camcorder that you only take with you when you're going somewhere special.

- It starts up quickly (because Paris isn't stopping for you) and it's simple enough that someone who has never seen it before can use it immediately.

- You don't need special software or cables to get your movie uploaded.

- And, finally, that the purpose of taking videos is to share them.

Stories manage to pack a lot of information into a few words. They're efficient. They're also easy to remember and to share, which means they're more likely to come up when you're discussing design decisions. In fact, people love stories so much that if you don't give them a story, they'll invent their own ("If I were using this camera, I would..."), which can drag your vision all over the place—so make sure it's your story they're using.

It's worth spending time to get the details of your story right; and if you're designing for simplicity, those details are especially important.

Imagine you're standing
on the street when...

Putting it all together

Don't worry too much about the form of your story. What matters is getting your constraints down on paper.

Keep your story minimal. Don't get sucked into describing events in detail. Instead, describe each goal and identify the feature that resolves it (the core features). There are three reasons for this. Firstly, a brief story is easier to remember and retell, so it's more likely to be used. Secondly, it's easier for people to imagine how that story could play out in other circumstances (so you can imagine handing your Flip camera to a parent at a kid's birthday party). Finally, adding detail into a story is like a movie camera zooming in: people assume that their attention is being drawn to something important. At best, this will feel odd; at worst, people will invent reasons why the detail matters. So only add details that matter and that help you explain the story.

Show, don't tell. We're used to trusting people's actions more than their words. Descriptions of users' behavior will make a stronger impression than assertions about their character. Don't say the protagonist is detail-oriented; mention that she cross-checks her work with her notes. Showing makes something concrete.

Don't invent. Your story needs to be credible, and to be credible it must be based on real people and real events. The Paris Hilton story I told about the Flip is based on something that really happened to a friend of mine. Your specific story might combine elements from several events, which is truthful even if it's not a true story. But unless your story is based on real events, you won't be able to back it up and it will feel artificial. Using relevant details, as described here, makes your story concrete and believable.

Practice it, say it aloud, tell it to someone else, refine it. Doing so will help you find and fix the flaws in your story and help you boil it down to the essentials. Soon, you will have a story you can tell in a few sentences that explains your vision.

A good user story is brief, concrete, credible, and uses relevant detail.

"Writing is hard work. A clear sentence is no accident. Very few sentences come out right the first time, or even the third time. Remember this in moments of despair. If you find that writing is hard, it's because it *is* hard."
—William Zinsser, *On Writing Well*

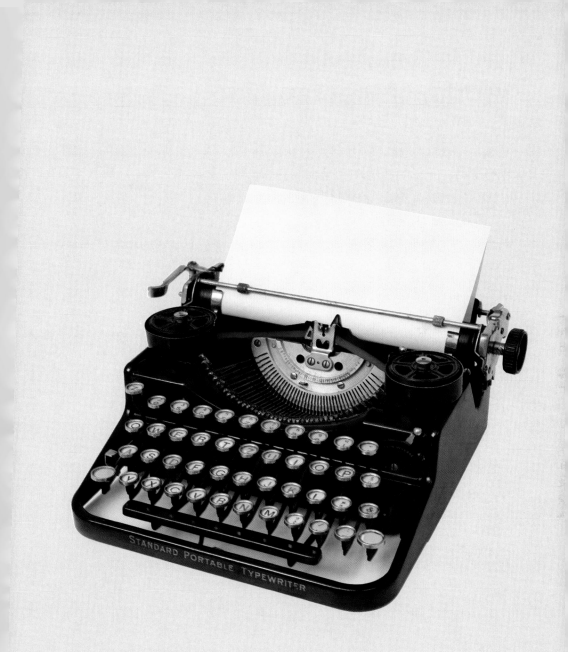

Now tell a story.

World, character, plot

If you look back at the vision we've developed, you'll see there are three levels.

- A believable world (the "where" and "when" of our story)
- Credible characters (the "who" and "why")
- A coherent plot (the "what" and "how")

Many designs feel complex because they don't take into account the pressures of the real world, because they expect the user to be able to cope with anything, or because they miss vital steps. Your design needs to fit comfortably into the complete story.

Michael Johnson, Moving Pictures Group Lead at Pixar, has described how Pixar uses this approach to creating movies. The movie is built from the outside in, starting with a world (toys are alive when people aren't around), adding characters and motives (a cowboy who's jealous of the new spaceman toy), and finally describing the plot (they fight and fall into the hands of a toy killer and have to cooperate to escape).

If they run into problems with the plot, they go back to the characters to understand what they would do. If they run into problems with the characters, they look at the world to see how it shapes them.

The same goes for our user experience story for the Flip camera. If you want to know how the person taking the movie would act, you need to look at who they are (someone who has never used the camera before) and the world they're in (a crowded street with no time to ask questions), so they'd be flustered and they'd look for one simple button to press.

Place your design within a plot, driven by credible characters and set in a believable world. In the words of architect Eliel Saarinen: "Always design a thing by considering it in its next larger context—a chair in a room, a room in a house, a house in an environment, an environment in a city plan."

World

Character

Plot

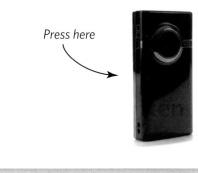

Press here

Extreme usability

When you look at stories of simple experiences, it's clear what sets *simple* experiences apart: they work under extreme conditions.

To be simple, you have to aim for something tougher than the regular goals for usability.

Usability aims for...	Simplicity aims for...
a specific group of people can use it	anyone can use it
easy to use	effortless to use
responds quickly	responds instantly
understood quickly	understood at a glance
works reliably	works always
straightforward error messages	error-free
complete information	just enough information
works in a user test	works in a chaotic environment

Targets like "instant" and "effortless" are intimidating because, in truth, they're unattainable. But there's an important benefit of shooting for a target you can't hit: it keeps you facing in the right direction.

Imagine setting a target of "responds quickly" instead of "responds instantly". It would be easy to justify making a change that would slow the response time down by only a second—after all, that's still "quick" isn't it?

Slowly, with each successive change, you find your design stops being simple and starts becoming slower and more irritating. Compromises like these happen all the time in design meetings and this is why the products we love often turn into monsters we loathe.

If, instead, you set a target of "instant," you find yourself looking for changes that make the experience quicker.

It's been pointed out that products that start out simple often end up getting so complex they cease to be useful. But if you set extreme targets, over time your product gets better (or at least achieves the goals that really matter).

Aiming for extreme targets, even ones you can't quite reach, will help you keep your product simple.

Designing simple experiences means reaching for extreme targets.

The quick and dirty way

The quick way to get to a vision often works when I'm making minor improvements or working on something small, like a single web page.

I begin by describing what I'm designing in plain language. I say it out loud to anyone who'll listen—I find it comes out better that way. If it sounds odd or the listener doesn't understand what I've just told them, then I know I need to rephrase it and try again, usually with someone new to whom I've not given any clues. If there's no one available, I'll write it down, but explaining it to a person is always best because their reaction tells you whether you're getting it right.

My aim is to come up with a description that is concise, clear, and complete.

I try to make it no more than one short sentence. If I can sum up the main activities without branching off into details or losing the listener's interest, then I know I've made it concise.

If the listener understands it right away, I've probably made it clear.

I don't try to list every feature. I just try to explain the main features at the same level of detail. If I can summarize the main points without leaving out important details, then I know I've made it complete.

For the Flip camera, the description is "take and share video." For a newspaper home page, it's "a summary of the most important events right now." Even a complicated device like the iPhone can be described by its core components: Steve Jobs introduced it as "a widescreen iPod..., a revolutionary mobile phone, and a breakthrough Internet communications device."

When I've done that, I make sure I set some constraints on the actions to focus me on making them as simple as possible. So for the Flip, that would be "take video instantly and share it effortlessly."

It normally takes a few iterations to get it right, but it always pays off because it helps me focus on what's important.

Describe what you want in the simplest possible terms.

Insight

The magic happens when you take the things that you've learned in researching your story and turn them into a deep understanding of the problem you're trying to solve.

The trick turns out to be simple. It only looks like magic when you've had enough time and practice to make it appear effortless.

- First, look back over the facts you've gathered about your users, the problems they face and the world they live in. Prioritize the things that have the most impact on your users' behavior. For instance, in my earlier example about the car dealers, interruptions from customers had a huge impact on the dealers' task of creating a marketing plan.

- Next, look for points in your story that you can act on. In the car dealers' example, we couldn't stop the interruptions, but we could make the tasks shorter and help users to pick up where they left off by giving them a checklist to complete.

- Now prioritize those points: where can you have the most impact? What can you change easily? For the car dealers, creating shorter tasks had the most impact on the dealers' ability to complete their marketing plans, so it became our top priority.

- Finally, test your insights. What would happen if your ideas weren't true? Is anything likely to change that will affect your insight? Can you see examples or counterexamples anywhere already? Do these reveal flaws in your insight or are there other reasons (for instance, a poorly executed design)?

Testing your insights means spending more time watching people in the real world, often using prototypes or competitors' products. This is where you find the small differences that make your insights valuable.

Spend time reviewing the data behind your story and discussing it.

Review your story and ask: What things have the most impact on your users' behavior?

Getting the right vision

Whether you take the long route or the quick and dirty route, writing a vision will take longer than you expect.

"As designers, we want to start designing immediately. It's important to resist that," says Jürgen Schweizer of Cultured Code. Starting design early means missing out on important insights. It can even mean designing the wrong thing entirely.

A few years ago, an automotive manufacturer asked me to design a car selector. They already had a design in mind: make it easy for people to choose a car by asking them questions about their lifestyle and personality, and then offer a shortlist.

When I tried out the idea on customers, they told me that their answers would be lies. "If I tell them that I have a dog, they won't let me see a coupé," one customer explained. Customers quickly became irritated by the convoluted process of finding a car by describing their hobbies.

It turned out that customers had a general idea of what they wanted. They could make a choice they were happy with if they were just given clear photos of a lineup of cars.

Spending time understanding the problem leads to better, simpler solutions.

> "When you start looking at a problem and it seems really simple, you don't really understand the complexity of the problem. Then you get into the problem, and you see that it's really complicated, and you come up with all these convoluted solutions. That's sort of the middle, and that's where most people stop.... But the really great person will keep on going and find the key, the underlying principle of the problem—and come up with an elegant, really beautiful solution that works."
>
> —*Steve Jobs (quoted in* Insanely Great: The Life and Times of Macintosh, the Computer that Changed Everything *by Steven Levy)*

As Luke Wroblewski, former Chief Design Architect at Yahoo!, says, "Your first design may seem like a solution, but it is usually just an early definition of the problem you are trying to solve."

In my experience, roughly the first third of any project is spent trying to figure out what's really important. It's a nerve-wracking time, as complexity seems to spiral and there's no solution in sight. Sticking with it is the first and most important step in achieving simplicity.

Don't rush into design. Understanding what's core takes time.

The really great person will keep on going... and come up with an elegant, really beautiful solution that works.

—Steve Jobs

Share it

In 2002, Alan Colville was a product manager at Telewest, a British cable TV company. He'd been charged with upgrading the set top box software, a job that touched on every part of the company's workforce, from software developers to call centers. As he described it:

> People at the company were pretty cynical about new projects and change was seen as a bad thing. Everything we'd done before was too complex, had needed fixing after it was released, and was irritatingly slow. We needed to show people that this project was going to be different in that it focused on our typical customers and their needs. Bringing this new focus, we wanted to deliver something that was the opposite of what we'd done in the past by being simple, stable, and fast.

Colville started putting up posters around the company, promising that the project was going to make the set top box "simple, stable, fast."

Those three words became the guiding principles for every decision: "Will it make the experience simpler, stabler, faster?" was a question that he asked at every meeting. Colville remembers:

> I knew it was working when I was on a conference call and a project manager was telling me about an idea that had been dropped. She told me, "It would have made it simpler and stabler, but not faster—so we're not going ahead with it."

> The stress just fell away and the design started to go right. Normally the company would hemorrhage money to customer support whenever there was a new software release. This time, when we released the software, our support call volume was negligible. We saved £3million on that alone.

Sharing your vision means that the right decisions get made even when you're not there. It means your stakeholders can tell the difference between good decisions and bad decisions.

Making your core statement visible reminds people how important it is. Using it all the time makes it second nature to them. Putting it in the public eye means everyone on the team knows they have to deliver what's expected of them.

Once you have found and begun sharing your vision, you're ready to design.

Repeat your story to everyone involved with the project, every time you meet them. Don't stop retelling your story. When you're getting bored of it, the message is just starting to get through.

Tell your story.

Part 3

Four strategies for simplicity

Simplify this

Whenever I invite someone for a job interview as a designer, I ask them to show me how they'd take something that seems unnecessarily complicated and simplify it.

For a long time, I've been giving people the task of simplifying a DVD remote control, because most people have one at home and because, as we'll see, it presents some tricky problems.

Typically, a DVD remote control has over forty buttons; many have more than fifty. That seems excessive for a device that's used to play and pause movies.

When something is that complicated, there should be plenty of scope for simplifying it. But the task turns out to be harder than you'd imagine.

Try it now: you can refer to your own DVD remote or use the template on the following page. You may find it helps to discuss the problem with a friend, but I wouldn't do this while they're trying to watch a DVD.

On/Off
Quick OSD (On-screen display menu)
FL Select (Change the display on DVD player)
Open/Close (Eject DVD)
Advanced Disc Review (Review playlist)
AV Enhancer (Adjust audio and video)
Repeat (Repeat play)
Multi Re-Master (Improve audio quality)
Numeric Keypad
Depth Enhancer (Reduce picture 'noise')
Manual Skip (Skip 30 seconds forward)
Quick Replay (Skip back a few seconds)
Cancel
Skip Forward
Skip Back
Slow Forward
Slow Back
Stop
Pause
Play
Direct Navigator/Top Menu (Main menu)
Play List/Menu (Show a disk menu or play list)
Functions (Change on-screen menu)
Return (Return to previous menu)
Up Arrow
Down Arrow
Left Arrow
Right Arrow
Enter
Subtitle
Audio (Change soundtracks)
Angle/Page (Change angle/advance still pictures)
Setup (Quick setup menu)
Play Mode (All/group/random play)
Play Speed (Change play speed)
Zoom
Group (Selects groups of items to play)

The remote control

You can use the template on the opposite page for your remote control. The descriptions are the same as in the instruction manual for my own DVD player, but I've added some explanation to a few of them. Most people would just have the icons on the remote control to go by.

Sometimes, solving one problem leads to others. Try to think about how you'd use your version of the remote control and the ways in which it might feel simple or more complicated to use. Don't stick with the first design you come up with. It's always better to make three or four quick sketches than to grow too attached to one idea. Once you've done that, you can select a favorite and try to complete it.

I've been collecting people's designs for a while. If you'd like to see some of them and add your design to the list, visit simpleandusable.com.

On/Off
Quick OSD (On-screen display menu)
FL Select (Change the display on DVD player)
Open/Close (Eject DVD)
Advanced Disc Review (Review playlist)
AV Enhancer (Adjust audio and video)
Repeat (Repeat play)
Multi Re-Master (Improve audio quality)
Numeric Keypad
Depth Enhancer (Reduce picture 'noise')
Manual Skip (Skip 30 seconds forward)
Quick Replay (Skip back a few seconds)
Cancel
Skip Forward
Skip Back
Slow Forward
Slow Back
Stop
Pause
Play
Direct Navigator/Top Menu (Main menu)
Play List/Menu (Show a disk menu or play list)
Functions (Change on-screen menu)
Return (Return to previous menu)
Up Arrow
Down Arrow
Left Arrow
Right Arrow
Enter
Subtitle
Audio (Change soundtracks)
Angle/Page (Change angle/advance still pictures)
Setup (Quick setup menu)
Play Mode (All/group/random play)
Play Speed (Change play speed)
Zoom
Group (Selects groups of items to play)

The four strategies

Over the years I've seen many ingenious solutions to the problem of simplifying a DVD remote, but I've found that they fall into four categories:

- Remove—get rid of all the unnecessary buttons until the device is
  stripped back to its essentials.

- Organize—arrange the buttons into groups that make more sense.

- Hide—hide all but the most important buttons behind a hatch so
  they don't distract users.

- Displace—create a very simple remote control with a few basic
  features and control the rest via a menu on the TV screen,
  displacing the complexity from the remote control to the TV.

Some people do a little of each, but usually they pick a primary strategy. Some use additional technology like touch-screen displays on the
remote control or the ability to wave at the TV, but these are just forms
of removing, organizing, hiding, or displacing.

As I've tried to simplify other devices and experiences, I've found that
the same four strategies keep cropping up in one form or another. The
strategies apply to both functionality and content. And the strategies
apply whether you're looking at something large, like an entire website,
or something small, like a single page.

Each of the strategies has its strengths and weaknesses, which I'll discuss in the following chapters. A big part of success comes in choosing
the right strategy for the problem at hand.

Remove

Organize

Hide

Displace

Part 4

Remove

Remove

According to a 2002 study by Standish Group, 64 percent of software features are "never or rarely used." Take a look at your DVD remote control and count the number of buttons that you've never touched. The same goes for almost any gadget or software you care to name. There are plenty of opportunities to simplify by removing.

Removing or omitting features can lead to successful products:

- Tumblr's blog service has a fraction of the functionality of sites like WordPress or Blogger, but three years after its launch, it was booming with over two million blog posts every day.

- The Lotus Elise started life as a back-to-basics sports car with no air-conditioning and a production run of eight hundred. Fifteen years later, it is still in production and tens of thousands of them have been sold.

- At launch, the iPhone had fewer features than competing phones from Nokia and RIM (makers of BlackBerry), but it was an instant hit.

- Basecamp, a project management extranet by 37signals, does a fraction of what extranet software like Microsoft SharePoint does, but *BusinessWeek* described it as "addictively easy-to-use" and it is used by millions of people worldwide.

Conventional wisdom says that more features mean more capability which, in turn, means a more useful product. But these examples choose depth of capability rather than breadth. They're useful because they do a few things far better than their rivals.

Conventional wisdom also says that products with more features will beat products with fewer. But all of these examples have competed against more fully featured rivals and won.

Removing clutter allowed designers to focus on solving a few important problems really well. It also allowed users to focus on meeting their goals without distraction.

It's often easy to understand what's essential: a DVD remote needs a play button and a stop button. The problem comes with things that might be valuable. So, when you're simplifying by removing, begin with a blank sheet of paper and ask, "What are the important problems?" Then gradually add the features and content that matter most.

The most obvious way to simplify is to remove what's unnecessary.

How not to do it

The wrong approach to removing features is getting rid of anything that's difficult to build.

A few years ago, I worked on a website that was intended to help people conserve electricity. The big idea was to let people track their electricity usage online and see how small changes in their habits could lead to big savings.

When it came time to begin the design, the project manager decided this feature was too difficult to deliver and dropped it in favor of publishing some articles about saving electricity. When the site launched, it looked substantial, but there was nothing compelling or original about it and it failed to gain the intended audience.

This is a common pattern. A deadline approaches, a budget tightens, and features are cut. Frequently, the team focuses on delivering as many features as possible. Those that are big or tricky to deliver are cancelled. If someone objects strongly, they're told their feature will be pushed into "phase 2" or "phase 3."

What's left behind often adds up to an uninspiring product that's similar to a lot of existing, mediocre offerings.

This approach can tear the heart out of a project and yet it's the standard approach to removing features and content, one I've encountered far more than any other.

You can't avoid the process of removing features and content. Every team has limited resources, and every design project I've encountered has reached the point where features or content needed to be cut. It might be a product that had grown too big over the years, or a new design that had to be reigned in.

Don't wait for the unsympathetic, unsatisfactory process of cutting the most interesting features. Take charge of the design and ensure that you're focusing only on delivering features and content that add value.

Cutting features can
be a bloody process.

Focus on what's core

Adding value begins with improving the core experience.

At Telewest, Alan Colville was asked to design a new set-top box incorporating a Personal Video Recorder (PVR).

With tight resources, Telewest couldn't deliver everything on its wish list, but the company was paralyzed over what to drop. So Alan started user-testing competitors' products to see what mattered to customers.

To his surprise, he found that customers were most concerned with one of the frustrations of recording. If they tried to record two TV shows, they couldn't watch a third. People complained that often they'd be recording two overlapping shows and wouldn't be able to change channels.

Overcoming this problem required adding a third TV tuner to the box—a major design change. But Alan's research showed that customers' frustration with this point was stronger than their interest in value-added features such as "red button" applications and interactive TV services, both of which had strong business cases but unproven customer need.

The research convinced the directors to switch their resources into the additional tuner. It quickly came to be seen as a competitive advantage and *Which?* (the UK equivalent of *Consumer Reports*) points to this flexibility as the box's major advantage.

When you're prioritizing features, remember that users value features that relate to their everyday experience of a product. Begin by following the path set in your vision story. For a PVR, the ability to record and watch TV is close to this everyday experience so it's more important than other features.

Users also value features that eliminate their frustrations effortlessly. When you're plotting your vision story, look for common frustrations and problems. Features that address these are your next priority. For a PVR, the ability to watch and record several shows at once turned out to be important enough to make it a priority.

Customers chose basic improvements over value-added extras.

Kill lame features

It's often a good idea to get rid of poorly implemented features. David Jarvis, Head of Online at TUI Ski, recalls that one of the websites he manages used to have features that let users filter search results and create shortlists. He says:

> Neither was implemented particularly well. Although both filtering and shortlisting are features we think should be part of the functionality, and although we'd got something that was kind of working, we felt we were giving people a half-baked experience. We took the features off the UK site and our conversion rate went up.

One objection to removing half-baked features or content is that the time and effort that has gone into creating them will be wasted. No matter how poor the item, if it's been paid for, no one wants to get rid of what they have. In the words of Jack Moffett, "Broken gets fixed. Shoddy lasts forever."

Economists call this the "sunk costs fallacy." In reality, the cost of creating the feature can't be recovered, so the only way to judge the feature is on how much good it is doing and how much more it will cost to keep.

Features and content always place a mental load on users ("Do I look at this or not?") and always cost something to maintain (someone will have to keep the content up to date or make sure the feature still works).

So the question is never, "Why should we get rid of it?" It is always, "Why should we keep it?"

Hanging on to features "because getting rid of them would be a waste" may be holding you back.

We tend to keep things, even when we know they're broken.

What if the user...?

If you've ever experienced design by committee, you know it can be impossible to argue that *anything* is unnecessary.

You start off with an idea of which features to kill, but, one by one, they are all justified with the words "but what if the user wants to...?" Sitting around a conference table, it's easy to imagine that, yes, a user might want to do just that. So the feature stays. By the time you get to the bottom of the list, you have most likely added a few more.

The "what if the user wants to...?" test allows any feature to get back into your product. If all a feature has to do is meet the "what if...?" test, then your plans will become choked with irrelevant junk. Like a traveler cramming his suitcase for every possible eventuality, you'll find yourself crushed beneath the weight of "what if...?"

It's fine to ask yourself "what if...?" when you mean "what if we solved the problem by...?" Dreaming up new ways of fixing things is one way to make your users' lives better.

What's *not* fine is using "what if...?" to dream up new problems or to guess at what's important to your users. Saying "what if the user wanted to...?" is a way of scaring people into imagining they have missed something. To cope with that fear, people are asked to divert time, effort, and money into adding features.

So "what if...?" can lead to fear that takes a powerful hold on meetings.

If you find yourself (or anyone else) saying, "What if the user needs to...?" there's only one answer: go find out whether it's really important to your users. Ask, "How often do the people I'm designing for encounter this problem?" If the answer is "hardly ever," then drop the idea and move on.

Stop guessing "what if...?" and go find out what *is*.

Avoid speculating about what users might or might not do.

But our customers want it

Jürgen Schweizer of Cultured Code warns against adding features simply because customers ask for them:

> We get a lot of feature requests, but what our customers don't always realize is that if we went ahead and put an idea straight into the product, we'd probably break it. It would be too much or we'd have to move something important. So we try to resist adding new features.
>
> Instead, we try to reverse engineer the ideas—to figure out what problem the customer was having and to think about whether or not it's something we should try to solve in our software.

Features often involve trade-offs that customers aren't always aware of. Letting applications run in the background on your mobile phone sounds good—until you realize how quickly that can drain your battery and how annoying it can be to find out which apps are running and turn them off manually.

Adding features doesn't always make the user's experience simpler. Often it can lead to more frustration.

Sometimes you may be able to come up with an alternative solution that meets customers' real needs (such as letting them switch between mobile applications quickly). But don't be afraid to ignore requests to add more to your product.

Hi there, Sign In to make a comment.

Share
Follow us on twitter

Ideas so far

Search Ideas

PRODUCT IDEAS

22,093 Coffee & Espresso Drinks
875 Frappuccino® Beverages
6,818 Tea & Other Drinks
9,931 Food
4,648 Merchandise & Music
6,421 Starbucks Card
6,814 Other Product Ideas

EXPERIENCE IDEAS

5,423 Ordering, Payment, & Pick-Up
9,326 Atmosphere & Locations
7,801 Other Experience Ideas

INVOLVEMENT IDEAS

3,002 Building Community
6,278 Social Responsibility
4,283 Other Involvement Ideas
374 Outside USA

QUESTION OF THE DAY

What's your "My Starbucks Rewards" level?
more info
○ Welcome
○ Green
○ Gold
○ Not a Member

Submit

Leaderboard

1. **tkfoss** | 656 Comments
2. **christann** | 236 Comments
3. **DanMark** | 212 Comments
4. **betterbefore** | 170 Comments
5. **Steve1** | 159 Comments
6. **pechipys1** | 157 Comments
7. **AgentDesmond** | 151 Comments
8. **iyogagirl** | 147 Comments
9. **thewhiterabbit** | 140 Comments
10. **Barista_Marie** | 112 Comments

SHARE.
VOTE.
DISCUSS.
SEE.

You know better than anyone else what you want from Starbucks. So tell us. What's your Starbucks Idea? Revolutionary or simple – we want to hear it. Share your ideas, tell us what you think of other people's ideas and join the discussion. We're here, and we're ready to make ideas happen. Let's get started.

Most Recent Ideas

51 Min(s) Ago	DIET FRAPPUCCINO
2 Hour(s) Ago	Those Extra Shots Fresh Idea
8 Hour(s) Ago	It's a WIN-WIN!
9 Hour(s) Ago	Give Target and Kroger (etc) Starbucks Baristas Partner Numbers!
9 Hour(s) Ago	Sell Highly Concentrated Chai in Stores!
10 Hour(s) Ago	Bring back blackberry flavoring for the green tea frappucinos!
10 Hour(s) Ago	Self service drip coffee in the mornings
10 Hour(s) Ago	Pike still sucks
11 Hour(s) Ago	Peanutbutter Mocha Frappuccino
11 Hour(s) Ago	Starbucks Dietitian

Featured Starbucks Idea Partners

These are our Starbucks Idea Partners. They'll be online to listen to your ideas, ask questions, tell you what we're doing behind the scenes and make sure things run smoothly.

sbx_jcar Jeff works with the Starbucks Card Mobile app. He loves MSI because it gives Starbucks a way to amplify the voices of our customers and partners while identifying business needs. : Estate Java (he's also quite partial to the new soy Coffee Light Frappuccinos)

sbx_nat Natalie manages the My Starbucks Rewards program from a technology perspective. She is currently working on bridging the current 'gap' we have with Licensed Stores. You can follow sbx_nat on Twitter: @starbuckscard : free syrups and free drinks

Ideas in Action

All the ideas below came from you, our customers. Click on each one to find out more.

SELL JAMAICAN BLUE MOUNTAIN COFFEE IN THE STORES
Fresh Fruit
separate brewed coffee line/card swiping
Flavored coffee
Stars per DRINK, not per transaction!
Carry in a coupon for a free drink??? Are you kidding me?
"Bank" Free Drink when Buying a LB of Coffee
Better blenders=less ice chunks
Bring Back the After 2 Program
Use Fake Breakfast Sandwich Displays

Listen to your customers. But don't take their suggestions at face value.

Solutions, not processes

When I was working for an online bank the manager in charge of savings accounts asked me to add a feature that would allow customers to divide their savings accounts into "pots" that they could name ("holiday," "gas bill," and so on). This would help customers to become more diligent savers by seeing what they were saving towards.

When I started to design the process, things quickly became complicated. For instance, when a customer added money into a savings account, he would need to add the money, and then move it into a pot—two steps instead of one. When someone else added money into the account they might not know about the pots and so the money would need to go in another "general" pot in the account.

It became even more complex when transferring money from the account. The customer had to specify which pot the money should come from. And if the customer transferred too much money from that pot, they might be denied, even if there was enough money in the rest of the account.

This kind of feature—one that leads to a flood of exceptions and details—always sets my alarm bells ringing.

So I went back to the problem we were trying to address: helping customers remember why they were saving.

I realized that if we allowed customers to name their savings accounts, we'd have a similar effect to naming pots. If customers wanted another pot, they could open another account. We could even start them off with two or three accounts and suggest names for them. Compared to the cost of implementing, explaining, and supporting the pot feature, naming accounts was quick and cheap to implement. And it was far easier for customers to understand.

If you design by focusing on process, you'll often find yourself drawn into creating features to handle exceptions, problems, and details. If you want to remove all this complexity, then step back, focus on the customers' goals, and ask yourself, "Is there another way to solve this problem?"

Insufficient funds

⚠️ **Insufficient funds in this pot**

You do not have enough money in the pot 'New TV'

Funds requested: £950
Funds available: £945
Shortfall: £5

You may have additional funds in other pots in your
Easy Saver account: 098765432

Would you like to transfer the shortfall from another pot?

Choose pot: ⬍ **Gas bill**

(Cancel)   (Transfer)

When a small change leads to complex processes, it's time to step back and find another solution.

When features don't matter

If you're trying to make an appealing product, getting rid of features seems risky, but it has long-term benefits.

In 2006, three researchers—Roland T. Rust, Debora Viana Thompson, and Rebecca W. Hamilton—conducted an experiment to see whether features or usability mattered most to customers.

They divided participants into two groups and asked them to choose between two digital video players—one with seven features, the other with twenty-one features. Participants from the first group were only allowed to read about the products before they made their choice. The second group got a chance to use one of the products (either the high-feature model or the low-feature one) before making their choice.

Two-thirds of participants in the "no use" group chose the high-feature model. But only 44 percent of participants who used the high-feature model went on to choose it—and they were less confident that they had made the right choice.

Their conclusion: feature lists sell so long as customers don't get a chance to use the product. But once consumers have used a product, their preferences change. Suddenly usability matters very much.

Today, word of mouth, user reviews, personal recommendations, and product trials are becoming more important than mass advertising. Customers find out about products from other users—people who've learned to value usability. There's a strong argument for cutting features, rather than piling them on.

Overburdening your product with features is likely to decrease mainstream users' satisfaction and hurt sales in the long run.

In the long run,
adding features is
a losing strategy.

Will it hurt?

Once a feature has been released, someone, somewhere will eventually use it. If users like it, they will change their behavior to take advantage of it. People become addicted to their favorite features, and they will be irritated when one is taken away, no matter how trivial the change.

But some addictions are easier to break than others. What matters most to your users is this: is your design best at solving their big problems? If it is, they will stick with you, even when they're inconvenienced by your changes.

Judging how much the removal of a feature will affect users is a delicate business. Simply asking people, "Would you like us to remove this feature?" always delivers a resounding "No!" No one likes the thought of getting less. Even people who never have and never will use the feature will want to keep it. The *idea* of features is often more appealing than the reality.

Instead, begin by assessing how close it is to the users' core goal.

If you're designing a mobile application to help salespeople organize their leads, removing a feature that changes the background color won't hurt: it's not a core task.

But if the feature is closer to the core of the application, things are a little harder.

Watching people use mock-ups is the best way to find out what really matters and to understand how they will respond.

Trying to please all users all the time is an impossible task. Aim to delight your target audience for their core tasks and hope to please them for the secondary tasks.

Some people find
it hurts more
than others.

Prioritizing features

When you're trying to figure out which features to keep and which to remove, follow these principles:

- Identify the users' goals and set them in order of priority. For the DVD remote control, the main goal is to watch the DVD; a secondary goal would be to use the DVD extras; a less important goal would be to play other media, like music CDs, MP3s, and so on.

- Focus on solutions that completely meet users' high-priority goals. Only then move on to the lower-priority goals.

- Identify things that are common sources of anxiety or stress and prioritize features that alleviate that stress effortlessly. For instance, interruptions (such as the telephone) are a common frustration when watching TV. The pause button on a DVD remote control is a way of minimizing that frustration.

- Identify the "good enough" controls that satisfy mainstream users' needs and the "precision" controls for experts. Set aside the "precision" controls. For instance, the DVD remote control in this book has four buttons that directly control fast-forwarding. Two controls (fast-forward and skip to the end of a chapter) would be good enough in almost all situations.

And finally, don't be tempted to judge the value of your product by the number of features. Instead, consider how well it meets users' high-priority goals.

Prioritize features that satisfy mainstreamers' needs with minimal effort.

Load

People have a limited capacity to process information, learn procedures, and remember details. And in the real world, they're under far more pressure from interruptions and deadlines than in a user-testing lab, which limits their capacity even more.

Small details in an interface can add to the load on the user and slow them down like speed bumps and potholes on a road.

When The Co-operative Bank asked my business partner, Richard Caddick, to increase the number of people clicking through their home page, he set out to reduce the load on people visiting the page.

- He removed text that was not being looked at, such as the tagline underneath the bank's name.

- He simplified the layout, removing a vertical column on the right side of the page so it was easier to see which items were important and which were low-priority.

- He eliminated duplicate links, such as the "Tell me about…" drop-down menu, cutting the number of clickable items by about 20 percent.

- He limited the number of styles used for buttons and links to make it easier to distinguish what was clickable and what was not.

- He reduced the number of promotional slots so there were fewer distractions for customers who knew where they were going.

- He cut down the visual clutter by removing distracting elements such as lines that were used to divide content and a horizontal yellow bar across the page.

This small project took just a few weeks to complete, but it resulted in a significant boost to the number of visitors clicking through the home page and going on to complete application forms.

Removing options, content, and distractions lightens the load on users so they can focus on getting the job done. Removing visual distractions helps them process what they're seeing faster and more reliably. It's the details that make all the difference.

Before

After

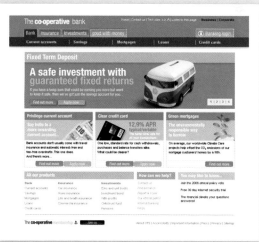

Decisions

We often focus on giving users as many choices as possible. But choice can easily overwhelm users.

In 2000, Dr. Sheena S. Iyengar and Dr. Mark R. Lepper set up a tasting booth at Draeger's Market in Menlo Park, California. Hundreds of people walked past the booth each day. One weekend, they put out a selection of twenty-four varieties of jams; on another they set out six. The wider selection performed badly. Only 2 percent of passersby bought the jam. When there were fewer options, 12 percent of passersby purchased the jam.

Iyengar and Lepper repeated similar experiments in a number of settings, and found that people were more likely to make a purchase when given a handful of choices than when they were overwhelmed with dozens of options.

They also found that people who were given a limited choice were more satisfied with their selection than those who'd been given more options.

Offering people a choice gives them a sense of control, and people prefer some choice to no choice. But when that choice exceeds a handful of options it becomes a burden, especially when the options are similar.

You can see something similar at work in people's attitudes toward technology. Most people are anxious when faced with a massive array of options and buttons. Every time they pick up a complex gadget, there's a nagging sense that they don't fully understand it, and that a slip of a finger could easily make things go wrong. People can easily distrust choice.

When you're next looking at a long feature list, a web page with dozens of links, or a computer menu that's full of choices, it's worth remembering how easily this choice can undermine your design.

Users are happier when their choices are limited.

Distractions

User interfaces, and web pages in particular, are full of irritating distractions. These can turn even simple tasks, such a reading a body of text, into a chore.

Hyperlinks within an article may seem like helpful extras, but each link says, "Why not stop what you're doing and look at this instead?" They break into the user's consciousness and undermine her concentration. Researcher Erping Zhu has found that increasing the number of hyperlinks within a document lowers readers' comprehension—even if the reader doesn't follow the link.

The right-hand column of a web page often is often set aside for even more distracting links. They're usually brightly colored and animated to attract the user's attention away from the main focus of the page.

Users may well click on the links, but if their journey ends in confusion, listlessness, or irritation, the distraction has been counterproductive.

Things have got so bad that Apple's Safari web browser now lets you remove these distractions so you can concentrate on reading.

The best place for these extras is at the end of a page where the user has finished reading. If users aren't reading that far, then it's a sign that the article itself needs work.

If you're designing simple experiences, your job is to remove distractions and let the user focus.

Before

After

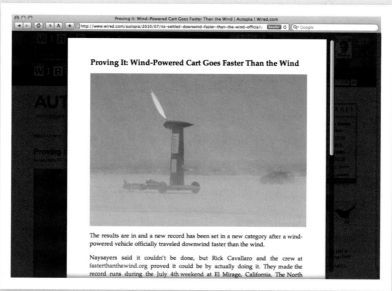

Smart defaults

You can reduce the number of decisions that a user has to make by choosing smart defaults.

Many car manufacturers' websites allow you to compare the model you're viewing with similar models. Click on the "compare" feature and you're asked to add two or three other models into a comparison chart. Lexus's European website doesn't do this. It prefills the table with the car you're researching and the two closest models. Often, the models it chooses are exactly the ones you need to make a useful comparison.

Some people may have to change the default selections, but they're no worse off than if the table were left blank. Overall, Lexus is saving time for its customers.

Smart defaults are ones that suit the largest possible number of people. Customer data, such as log files, provides a wealth of useful information for smart defaults.

- Popular documents ("Top news stories")
- Similar items ("Customers like you looked at...")
- Personal information ("Auto-fill the form with your address")
- Common choices (Putting "USA" at the top of an alphabetical list of countries because most of your customers come from there)

It's worth remembering that when a customer returns to a website or an application, he frequently wants to pick up where he left off.

- Recently saved documents ("Open hello-world.doc")
- Resume a process ("Continue your game from level 3")

A complaint I hear frequently from users of travel websites is how tedious it is to re-enter the same information every time they visit. Imagine how much simpler it would be if travel sites remembered the routes you typically fly or the hotels you usually visit.

Defaults are a powerful way of saving users time, effort, and thought, and a great way to remove speed bumps from your design.

Lexus's default comparisons are useful for most customers, most of the time.

Options and preferences

When you're looking for something to remove, options and preferences are a good place to begin.

In general, options help users to customize their setup. This is classic expert behavior—experts want to get under their car and tinker with it, mainstreamers want to get in and drive.

I've found that options and preferences generally creep into designs when the design team isn't sure what to do. Maybe there are two possibilities for navigating a website: breadcrumb links or drop-down menus. Both look good, so both go in. That way the user has a choice.

This sounds like it would be helpful, but should users be wasting their time figuring out which navigation technique is most convenient? That task is so far removed from a vision of a simple product that it never appears. Let's go back to the Paris Hilton story for a minute. Imagine: you hand your camera to a friend who then determines which of the three available grip positions and shutter buttons is best. Your friend would be wasting precious time, and you'd probably miss your chance to take the video.

Simple user experiences don't force the user to make these kinds of choices. It's the responsibility of the design team to do that. The best way to decide is to try it out on some users. And if there's no clear winner, and no dangerous pitfalls, then there's no "wrong" design. Choose which one to implement and move on.

View

◀ ▶   Back/Forward   Show All   🔍 Search Word Preferences

Show

☑ Drawings   ☑ Highlight
☐ Object anchors   ☐ Bookmarks
☐ Field codes   ☐ Text boundaries
Field shading: [When selected ⬍]   ☐ Image placeholders
☑ Comments on rollover   ☐ Draft font
☐ Background colors and images in Print Layout View   ☑ Contact Tags

Nonprinting characters

☐ Tab characters   ☐ Optional hyphens
☐ Spaces   ☐ Hidden text
☐ Paragraph marks   ☐ All

Window

☑ Status bar   ☑ Horizontal scroll bar
☑ Live Word Count   ☑ Vertical scroll bar
☑ Vertical ruler   ☐ Wrap to window
Style area width: [0 cm] ⬍

Description of preference

Show Object anchors
Displays object anchors, which indicate that an object is attached to a specific paragraph. Object anchors are visible only when the All check box is selected or when you click the Show/ Hide button on the Standard toolbar to display nonprinting characters. This does not affect Draft or Outline views.

[Cancel]   (OK)

Mainstream users don't like the burden of setting options and preferences.

When one option is too many

Sometimes, even one option is too many. A while back I watched a user test of the special offers section of a travel website. We asked participants to find and book a holiday. They easily found holidays that they wanted and announced they had made a decision. But next to the booking button was a link to "look for more deals." This proved irresistible. Every time a participant came close to booking, she clicked that link. No one booked a holiday.

We'd assumed that the link would help people who weren't quite sure. Instead, it undermined the confidence of everyone who came close.

When you're offering a choice to your users, think very carefully about whether you're overwhelming them with options or undermining their confidence in their decision.

Take a look at the design of the online checkout on any big site like Amazon or Best Buy. The checkout is where users have to make a choice: buy or bail. The retailers know that any doubt will undermine users' willingness to complete the transaction. So in the checkout, retailers remove navigation links that are normally at the top and bottom of every other page.

I doubt most customers are aware that this happens; when they get to those pages, they're too busy filling in forms. But retailers know that if they put those links back, customers will click on them and the sale will be lost. If this seems somehow underhanded, consider whether it is in the customers' interest to waste time by constantly dithering between website and checkout.

Remember, mainstreamers want "good enough, quickly;" experts want "perfect in as long as it takes." If you're designing the kind of simple experience that mainstreamers love, then ask yourself if the options you're giving them will sacrifice speed and simplicity for perfection. If the answer is "yes," remove the options.

What you mean

Browse other choices | Buy now

What they see

Keep my options open | No turning back

Errors

Even small errors can add to the load on users. They're an opportunity to simplify a user experience.

A few years ago I was asked to design a current account display for an online bank. The bank wanted the service to match their brand values: friendly, approachable, and simple.

On the current account screen was a control that allowed the user to choose a bank statement. The user selected the month and year of the statement from two drop-down menus and clicked "Go." It seemed simple enough.

But the control could generate two possible error messages. If you selected a date in the future, an error message came up that said, in effect, that you'd been stupid. If you selected a date that was over a year old, you were told to try again, since the bank only kept statements for a year. A person in a hurry could easily make either mistake, and neither error message was particularly friendly, approachable, or simple.

The problem was that the user was being asked to enter a date, when really he needed to choose from the last twelve bank statements. So I replaced the two date controls with a single drop-down list of the available bank statements.

With the redesigned control, users could only select from what was available, so there were no error messages to design. This made the system simpler to maintain, too.

Whenever a user has to correct an error, it breaks his concentration and makes the experience feel more complex. Designers often try to prevent errors by interrupting the user ("Are you sure you want to do that?"), but in a way this approach is worse because it interrupts everyone, whether they've made a mistake or not.

When you're trying to simplify an experience, looking for places where error messages are needed, or checking the error logs for common error messages, is a critical step.

Removing sources of errors is an important way to simplify an experience.

If you forget to change the year, you can accidentally request next month's bank statement. The redesigned interface simply lists the available bank statements.

Before

November ▼ | 2010 ▼ | GO

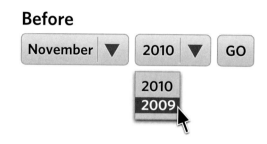

2010
2009

After

September 2010 ▼

August	2010
July	2010
June	2010
May	2010
April	2010
March	2010
February	2010

Visual clutter

Removing visual clutter means people have to process less information and can concentrate on what's important on the page. I've noticed that users describe interfaces they like as "clean," meaning free from clutter.

The designer Edward Tufte talks about needing to make the "data-ink ratio" as high as possible. In other words, ink (or pixels) shouldn't be wasted on anything that isn't content or in repeating content. So he removes the gridlines on graphs, leaving just the axes and the zigzag line of the graph itself. He reasons that the gridlines distract the reader from the important data: the shape of the graph.

The process for removing clutter is simple. Look at each element in the design and ask why it is needed. Is it critical information or there for support? Try to remove it from the design. If the design no longer works, replace the element.

Here are some good ways to limit visual clutter:

- Use white space or subtle background tints to divide up the page rather than lines. Why? Because lines sit in the foreground, so you pay more attention to them than tints or white space that sit in the background.

- Use the minimum possible emphasis. Don't make something bold, large, and red, if simply making it bold will do.

- Avoid thick dark lines where fine, light lines will do.

- Limit the levels of information. If you have more than two or three levels of information on a page you may be confusing the user. For instance, limit the number, sizes, and weights of fonts. Try to keep to just two or three levels in total, e.g., a headline, subheading, and body text.

- Limit the variation in sizes of elements. For instance, if you're designing an online newspaper, you might have a large block of text for the main story and five smaller blocks of text for secondary stories, rather than six blocks of text in different sizes.

- Limit the variation in shapes of elements. Stick to one button style rather than using three or four different ones.

You'll be surprised how much clutter you can remove from a page.

Before

After

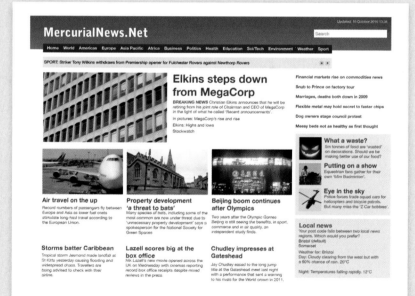

Removing words

Why are so many web pages clogged with words that no one will ever read? Perhaps it's because, unlike paper, web pages can always accommodate more text, so it costs nothing to add another paragraph or two. Or three.

The extra text is often wasted. Users don't slavishly read every word. Their eyes skim over pages, picking out the odd keyword or sentence.

Getting rid of text has three benefits:

- It makes what's important stand out.

- It reduces the effort it takes to interpret a screen.

- It makes people more confident that they've understood what's there.

When you're hunting for text to cut, be aware of some common hiding places:

Skip the introductions. Often the opening text on home pages and in articles says nothing at all ("Welcome to our web site, we hope you'll enjoy…"). It doesn't sound chatty or inviting, it just leaves the reader wondering where the author is heading. Cut the intros and start with a bang.

Delete unnecessary instructions. These are frequently redundant and can be cut completely. Delete text like "Fill in the fields in this form and press Submit to send your application to us." The page title ("Application Form") and the contents of the page (a form) are enough to signal the user what to do.

Simplify explanations. Sometimes links have descriptions under them. These can be useful, for instance, when one audience expects the link to be called one thing and another expects it to be called something else. But often, explanations are another source of redundant text. Replace "Product Finder: Answer some simple questions and we'll find the right product for you" with "Product Finder," and you'll save twelve words from a total of fourteen.

Use descriptive links. Links called "Click Here" or "More" sometimes appear under the headlines that describe exactly where they go. Simplify the page by using the headline itself as the link.

> "Get rid of half the words on each page, then get rid of half of what's left."
> —Steve Krug's Third Law of Usability from *Don't Make Me Think! A Common Sense Approach to Web Usability*

START CROSSING

WATCH FOR
TURNING VEHICLES

FLASHING

DO NOT START

FINISH CROSSING
IF STARTED

STEADY

DO NOT CROSS

TO CROSS →

PUSH BUTTON

Avoid unnecessary
instructions.

Simplifying sentences

Almost any sentence can be simplified and almost any text can be cut. In *Revising Prose*, Richard Lanham offers a simple method to turn long-winded writing into short, crisp sentences.

■ Circle the prepositions (of, in, for, onto, into, about). They drain the action from a sentence, so try to eliminate them.

■ Circle the "is" verb forms ("is taking time") and replace as many as you can ("takes time").

■ Convert passive voice ("time is needed for this project") into active voice ("this project needs time").

■ Cut out slow starts ("One can easily see that…") and get to the point.

■ Eliminate redundancies. Don't say "on a daily basis" when "daily" means the same thing.

These rules make text clearer, more persuasive, and shorter.

For example:

■ Please note that although Chrome is supported for both Mac and Windows operating systems, it is recommended that all users of this site switch to the most up-to-date version of the Firefox web browser for the best possible results. (41 words)

Simplified version:

■ For best results, use the latest version of Firefox. Chrome for Mac and Windows is also supported. (17 words)

Use Lanham's rules to remove the words that pad your sentences.

DDB UK's advertisement for Volkswagen in the UK shows just how much you can cut.

~~Our~~ BlueMotion ~~range combines lighter materials, enhanced aerodynamics, economical engines and tyres that create less friction, which~~ saves you ~~fuel and can reduce your tax, which means you will have more~~ money.

BLUEMOTION — TECHNOLOGIES —

Another example of ~~Volkswagen~~ efficiency.

Das Auto.

Removing too much

In the Apple Store in Tokyo you'll find a remarkable glass elevator, finished in Apple's trademark brushed aluminum. What makes this elevator unlike almost any other in the world is that there are no buttons: none to call the elevator, and none inside. The lift shuttles between the four floors of the store, stopping at each one it passes.

Apple has reduced the elevator to its core: a platform for taking people between levels. But instead of feeling simple, it feels wrong. The elevator leaves you feeling unsettled, frustrated, and anxious. Will it stop at the floor I want? Why is it stopping when no one is getting on or off?

Apple has removed a crucial ingredient: control.

Without the sense of control (calling and directing the elevator) or the sense that a visible person is in control (the guy in front who just pushed a button for your floor) and the feedback that it's working (the button that illuminates when you push it), all you can do is hand yourself over to the machine and hope.

In the buttonless elevator, people waste time and attention worrying. Removing all control doesn't simplify the experience, it complicates it.

I've come across the same problem trying to get information from flight maps on airplane video screens. They switch from world map to local map to flight data agonizingly slowly. Not having any control makes that wait seem even longer.

People need to feel in control. They prefer to be pilots rather than passengers. When they're at the mercy of chance or hidden forces, they become so anxious that they invent superstitious behaviors that help them regain a sense of being in charge, like avoiding the cracks in the pavement or wearing a "lucky" shirt.

The trick is to give people control over outcomes. In other words, enough control to stop them from worrying that their basic needs won't be met, but not so much that they're wasting time making choices they don't need to make. (How fast should the elevator travel? How long should the doors stay open?)

No buttons in this elevator. But people prefer to be pilots, not passengers.

You can do it

Can a team within a large organization create a radical website design and convince stakeholders to remove content and features?

"The old home page was a billboard," says Fran Dattilo, the project manager for Marriott's 2009 home page redesign. "Everyone said, 'It's too cluttered, you've got to change it,' and everyone thought that their stuff had to stay on the new home page."

Marriott's user testing said the home page was a members-only club. It worked fine for regular customers, but newbies got lost and confused.

The home page redesign had to be flexible, but the user experience team discovered they'd created a monster that had grown out of control. They set about creating a design that was deliberately inflexible.

There were fewer content areas and only one featured item—the top item on a fan of cards. This slashed the number of links on the home page from 77 to 43, a big reduction in clutter.

To convince the company, the team gathered evidence. The new home page was the most tested design Marriott had ever launched, backed up with data from the live site. "We went back to our main stakeholders, and we could tell them that this link only got 500 clicks a year and that the new design worked in China as well as the U.S."

Even so, launch was stressful, recalls Mariana Cavalcanti, Marriott's Director of User Experience. "We came in at 3:30 in the morning to watch it go live. We had prepared the company for a 10 to 15 percent dip in bookings at first—that was important. But there was no dip. Satisfaction scores did fall—our regular users didn't see any need for change. But four months later satisfaction was above our previous levels. We still see a lot of comments on message boards comparing us to similar brands. We've made them look ugly."

Simple design is often said to be the work of a single visionary designer, a "ruthless" or "uncompromising" innovator. But most of us work in organizations where there's a lot of political give-and-take. Marriott shows you can simplify with a shared vision, a focus on the mainstream user, and a thoroughly researched design.

Before

After

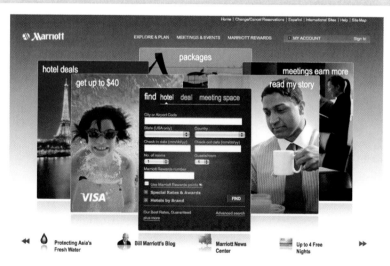

Focus

The "remove" strategy is about removing distractions to bring focus to your project:

- Focus on what's valuable to users. This means concentrating on features that deliver the users' core experience. It also means delivering features that eliminate users' frustrations and ease their sense of anxiety.

- Focus your resources on delivering value by removing lame features, irrelevant extras, and bribes.

- Focus on meeting users' goals. Agonizing over the process will get you bogged down in detail.

- Remove the distractions of tiny speed bumps that add to the load on the user: error messages, irrelevant text, unnecessary choices, and visual clutter.

With patience and the data to back you up, you can bring focus to most projects. If your problem is political, you can overcome it by building on small successes or by using evidence from tests. If your problem is out-of-date technology or incompatible systems, these too can change (slowly) over time. However, there are a couple of exceptions.

Sometimes there is an unavoidable legal requirement to include partic-ular wording or information. Financial services and medical regulations often require that specific wording is used, not because it makes sense to the public, but because it makes sense to lawmakers. Laws can be changed, too. David Sless in Australia has had some success in getting lawmakers to focus on whether consumers understand labels, rather than requiring long and confusing instructions.

Sometimes you can't remove because your design is part of a larger system. That's the case with the DVD remote. For instance, there are millions of DVDs in circulation that make use of the numeric keypad on the remote. If you removed it, you would risk breaking the user experi-ence for anyone who already owned such a DVD.

While you're waiting for the world to change, however, there are other ways of simplifying that are less radical, but quicker to implement.

**Removing clutter
helps users focus on
what's important.**

Part 5

Organize

Organize

Organizing is a great strategy for simplifying. In the case of the DVD remote control, it's probably the solution I've seen most often. It's usually an inexpensive solution—changing the layout and labeling the buttons on the DVD remote control costs less and demands fewer tough decisions than, say, removing.

There are plenty of options open to you in organizing an interface—size, color, position, shape, hierarchy. But those choices need to be employed with restraint. Some of the DVD remote controls I've seen over the years have had so many colored buttons they look as though they're made from Skittles.

If you want to organize for simplicity, it's important to emphasize just one or two important things. Simple organization doesn't draw attention to itself, it lets users focus on what they're doing.

The best DVD remote control designs emphasize the starting point (the on/off switch) and the most frequently used buttons (play, pause, and stop).

The Flip is also an excellent example of this. Of its nine buttons, only one (record) is strongly emphasized. If design is like a conversation, then openings are always the most difficult part. The Flip knows just how to say, "Hello, let's start here."

Organizing is often the quickest way to make things simpler.

Chunking

One way to make the blocks of buttons on the DVD remote control more manageable is to break them into chunks.

Chunking is used throughout user interface design. Microsoft Word has hundreds of features. To make them manageable, they are divided up into around nine menus. Each of those has a couple dozen commands—still too many to take in at a glance, so they're divided into chunks again. Click on a menu item and it'll often take you into a dialog box where even more features are available. The daunting list of features is grouped into manageable chunks within a hierarchy.

The classic advice here is to break items down into groups of "seven plus or minus two." In theory, this corresponds to the number of items your brain can hold in short-term memory. If you read a list of ten items, you'll likely have forgotten one of them by the time you get to the end.

Many psychologists now believe short-term memory may be rather smaller—perhaps just four items. But the "seven plus or minus two" rule remains, because it works. It seems to be a number that people can cope with. When I ask users to divide items into chunks, they tend to come up with around half a dozen groups.

There's no reason you can't divide the user's options into fewer chunks. I would always use as few chunks as feels simple to your mainstream user—fewer chunks mean fewer choices and less load on the user.

You don't always need to chunk. If your user needs to find an item in a long alphabetical list or timeline, there's no point in breaking up the list into half a dozen bits. Marking out letters of the alphabet or months of the year can help users to quickly scroll to approximately the right place, but chunking is most effective when users have to evaluate several possibilities rather than locate an item on a continuous index or scale.

**Organize into
bite-size chunks.**

Organizing for behavior

The first question a user will ask is, "What can I do with this?" so your first point of organization is to understand users' behavior: what they want to do and in what order they want to do it.

An online supermarket requires users to find the items they want to buy, add them to a shopping basket, schedule a delivery, and pay for the goods. Those are the main chunks into which the site should be divided.

People expect to begin their shopping by choosing groceries. This is also the most time-consuming part of the task, so it should be the most prominent.

People usually expect to do things in a particular sequence. It's disorienting and frustrating to break that sequence. The usual culprits here are registration processes and eligibility checks. If you can't remove them, defer them; if you can't defer them, minimize them. Find out what sequence of tasks users expect and do everything you can to stick to that pattern.

If your audience breaks down into totally separate groups who do completely different things on your website (like "doctors" and "patients"), this can be a useful first step.

The problem is that many audiences have similar or overlapping tasks. If your company provides information for journalists on its website, you'll need to give them company background information, press releases, new product information, press photographs, annual reports and staff biographies. A financial analyst wants almost the same information. If you don't have unique audiences, you probably shouldn't label by audience.

Mapping users' behavior will help you see how to organize your software.

Hard edges

When you need to organize a group of items that are equivalent (like books in an online store), choose clear categories with labels that make sense to your audience.

When I first started working on Peugeot's website, information about each car was organized into features (fitted as standard), options (fitted by the dealer), and accessories (fit yourself).

This made perfect sense to the company, but when I asked them to sort a CD player, electric wing mirrors, and an automatic gearbox into those categories, they couldn't agree.

The features, options, and accessories categories indicated whether something was standard—something only an insider could possibly know. If you organize items by a quality, you'll often run into these kinds of problems because users make different choices depending on their point of view.

Another way to organize the information would have been to sort it by type, such as comfort, technology, and storage. But these categories also depended on the user's point of view. For some customers, climate control was technology, for others it was comfort.

Simple organizational schemes have clear boundaries—hard edges—so that users know exactly where to find what they're looking for. Ask a handful of users to sort items into the categories. If they come up with different answers, or if they can't easily decide, you're in trouble.

Because cars are physical objects, I decided to use the layout of the car to organize the information: interior, exterior, and performance. All the customers knew where the CD player, the wing mirrors, or the automatic gearbox belonged.

Sometimes, you'll come across something that belongs in two categories. Too much duplication leads to confusion, but sometimes it is unavoidable. Tomatoes are a fruit, but you normally find them among the vegetables at a supermarket, so they must appear in both categories. The simplest categorization is usually the one with the fewest duplicates.

Features

Options

Accessories

**Good categories have
hard-edged distinctions.**

Alphabets and formats

There's an old joke: where does "finish" come before "start"?
In the dictionary.

Alphabetizing a list jumbles items up. So while alphabetical lists look simple, they're often hard to use. If users don't know the correct word for what they're trying to find, they're lost. Are you looking for a jacket or a sport coat? Do you want to speak to someone in Marketing or Sales and Marketing? Alphabetical lists work well for indexes of proper nouns—where there's a "correct" word to describe something—like surnames or countries. Otherwise, there are usually better alternatives.

Arranging content by format (words, pictures, videos) is another way of categorizing that looks simple but turns out to be unhelpful in the real world. If you're reading about Hawaii, you want to see photos and videos then and there. Going back to the start to find videos is just too much work.

The only situations I've come across where organizing by format makes sense are conference programs in which some formats, like tutorials, require a different registration process. In other words, some formats were used differently by the participants. But these are exceptions—it's usually simplest to organize conference information by time.

Alphabetizing often jumbles items up.

Search

There are a couple of big myths surrounding search and simplicity.

The first is that some users find searching easier than browsing—that there's a subgroup of people who always prefer to search. It's one of those myths that feels right. However, when Jared Spool tested a group of 30 users in over 120 shopping tasks, he didn't find a single individual who always preferred to search.

Instead, he found that when websites didn't offer links that looked like a good bet, users would search. That's not so surprising when you consider how much effort it is to think of an exact search term, type it in, and pick out a helpful search result. It's much easier to click on a link that looks like it'll carry you in the right direction. Browsing requires less mental effort up front; people will usually take the path that avoids having to think too much.

The exception is when you're asking people to pick one known item from a very large number of similar items, such as a specific track from the millions of downloadable tracks on iTunes. In this situation, yes, people will tend to search. In that case, browsing is more daunting than searching.

One of the hidden benefits of browsing is that when people look over the main links on a website, or the controls on an interface, they get an idea of what the software can do. Who needs introductory help messages when the interface speaks for itself?

The other myth is that designing a search is easier than organizing links to content. Perhaps it's because sites like Google make search look effortless that we assume it is easy to do. My experience is that it's harder to create a simple search interface. You need to take into account spelling mistakes and synonyms in users' search terms. Also, the search results themselves need to be organized. Take a look at a Google results page and you'll see a sophisticated layout that has been chosen to match the contents of your search.

If you're designing a simple user experience, it's usually best to begin with the basic organization and then move on to designing search.

Search is often harder to use and harder to design than browse.

Time and space

Setting events on a timeline is simple and powerful. It works best if the events are of similar duration so that users don't find themselves zooming in and out of a timeline or calendar very often. Although there may be other ways to organize the same content (such as conference themes), organizing events by time gives your audience a clear way to make sense of things.

Physical objects like hotels and countries can all be organized by space, as long as the users are familiar with the layout. For instance, you can organize a hotel website by an imaginary walkthrough of the hotel: concierge, front desk, dining, meetings and events, gym, rooms, suites. People have reasonably good memory for spaces, so this is often a good choice.

Visualizing time and space in diagrams can create some problems.

If you're plotting company offices or holiday destinations, you have to cope with the fact that some areas, like Europe, will be very crowded while others, like the Pacific Ocean, will be almost empty. The same goes for plotting events on a day planner (not much happens between 1:00 a.m. and 5:00 a.m.).

Sometimes it's useful to see variations in density, such as seeing that there's a concentration of bus services around rush hour. Other times, it can make information hard to pick out. I can set my computer's clock by clicking on a map of the world—but Paris and London are just a few pixels apart, even though they're in different time zones.

6:10p		C16
8:30p	On Time	A18
5:50p	On Time	A56
5:30p	On Time	A64
5:45p	On Time	C27
6:30p	On Time	A7
6:30p	On Time	A69
8:40p	On Time	A76
6:30p	On Time	C19
6:00p	On Time	

Timelines are a universal way of organizing events.

Grids

It's remarkable how far a tidy layout can go in making a design feel simple.

The form on the opposite page (top) is an interface for searching for train tickets that my company designed. It worked fine in user testing, but people hesitated over it. We revisited the layout and decided we could simplify it. We looked at the number of imaginary horizontal gridlines that were used to line up the field and simplified them. We also got rid of the heavy blocks of color that marked out the areas of the field and let the white space and alignment to the imaginary grid do the job.

The result was a layout that felt simpler to use, even though we hadn't changed the labels or programming of the form at all.

Lining items up using an invisible grid like this is an effective way of drawing the user's attention across the screen. It says, "Here's where to look next," without relying on bright colors or flashing images. The simpler the grid, the more powerful the effect.

Having even a few elements out of position can spoil a grid. In the example opposite, only three of the seventeen controls were out of position, but this was enough to disrupt the layout.

Grid layouts can feel regimented and constricting. One way around this is to make the layout asymmetric—for instance, by having an odd number of columns. Another is to have a few elements that straddle several columns. Take a look at websites and magazines like Wired or the _Guardian_ online and you'll see they're really designed around a regular, asymmetric grid.

Before

Out

| 5 ⬍ | February ⬍ | 🗓 |

| Depart ⬍ | 08 ⬍ | 30 ⬍ |

○ Just one way

Return

○ Anytime / Undecided <u>What's this?</u>

| 5 ⬍ | February ⬍ | 🗓 |

| Depart ⬍ | 08 ⬍ | 30 ⬍ |

Adults 1 ⬍   Children 0 ⬍

<u>Railcard</u>
<u>& other discounts</u>   None ⬍   <u>help</u>

After

Out

| February ⬍ | 05 ⬍ | 🗓 |

| Arrive ⬍ | 08 ⬍ | 30 ⬍ |

☐ Just one way

Return

☐ Anytime / Undecided <u>what's this?</u>

| February ⬍ | 05 ⬍ | 🗓 |

| Arrive ⬍ | 08 ⬍ | 30 ⬍ |

Passengers

| 1 ⬍ | Adults |

| 0 ⬍ | Children |

| 0 ⬍ | <u>Railcard</u> <u>& other discounts</u> |

Size and location

When you're laying out items on your grid, here are some tips for size and positioning.

Make important things big, even if that means making them out of scale. The illustration opposite is similar to one featured in one of the first books on interface design I read—Apple's *HyperCard Stack Design Guidelines.* If you're designing a sports news website, then making the golf ball as large as the soccer ball may not be accurate, but the alternative would be to make it look as though the Masters was less important than MLS. Sports fans can debate that, but sports editors would prefer to give them equal prominence.

Less important items should be smaller. Emphasize the difference in importance as much as you can, otherwise the user will get distracted. A good rule is: if something is half as important, make it a quarter as big.

Put similar things close together. This may sound obvious, but the benefits are huge. By placing similar items near each other, you reduce the need for visual clutter (such as color coding, labels, or boundary boxes) to explain how they are related. You also make it easier for users to focus their attention, because they don't have to look all over the screen.

When it comes to laying out navigation on computer screens, I've never seen any real evidence that navigation bars work better across the left- or the right-hand side of the screen or across the top—certainly not for websites. What really matters is that users can easily find the buttons they want, and for websites that often means putting the important links right in the middle with the content.

However, for touch interfaces it can matter a lot. Putting an app's navigation at the bottom of the screen means users can touch it without covering up the screen with their hand. On large touch screens, putting navigation on the left or right risks causing problems for right- or left-handed people respectively.

Distorting the ball sizes shows that each sport is equally important.

Layers

The London Tube map crams a lot of information into a very small space. Over three hundred stations on thirteen lines are squeezed onto a pocket-sized map. One way the map stops all this information getting jumbled up is by using a technique called perceptual layering.

Each tube line has a distinct color and so seems to sit on its own layer. Without noticing, readers tune in to the color of the line they're interested in and exclude other lines from their conscious thought. Although the map is a knot of different lines, the different colors allow readers to focus on just one at a time.

You can use perceptual layering to place several elements on top of each other or alongside each other; for instance, you might use a colored tint area to connect related content. Or you can tie together elements that are scattered across a user interface, making the buy button the same color as the shopping basket icon. If you use perceptual layers, you don't have to divide an interface into strict zones.

Perceptual layers work well with colors, but the same trick can be used with shades of gray, size, or even shapes.

Some tips:

- Use as few layers as possible. The more complex your content, the fewer layers you can get away with.

- Consider putting some basic elements on a general background layer, because it can be difficult to put one item on two layers.

- Make the difference between each layer as great as possible. Readers will struggle to tell the difference between 20 percent gray and 30 percent gray. Likewise, think of color-blind users when you're choosing colors.

- For categories that are more important than others, use bright, saturated colors to make them pop off the page.

- For categories that are equally important, use perceptual layers with the same brightness and size but vary the hue (like the lines on the London Tube map).

A quick way to figure out if your design is working is to squint at the screen and see if the layers are distinct.

UNDERGROUND

Reg. user No. 10/1806/P, Correct at time of going to print 08.2010

Color coding

Color coding is widespread. You see it in hospitals, folders, traffic lights, size charts, maps, dashboards—everywhere.

Perhaps because designs like the London Tube map are so successful, we tend to think color coding is a route to simplicity. But using colors to layer information is subtly different from using color to label information.

Layering information using color takes advantage of the way the mind works, so it places very little load on the user. But using colors to label information comes with a cost: like all codes, it takes time to learn and decode, so it requires extra effort from the user.

Casual visitors may not have time to learn your code. The more colors you use, the longer it will take to learn. And if you are not rigorously consistent in using the colors throughout your design, users won't be sure what the code means.

Another problem is in taking a system that's well known in one context and using it elsewhere. For instance, some British food labels include traffic light colors to suggest whether they contain items like salt or fat that people need to limit. While the traffic light colors are familiar to drivers, their meaning needs to be explained all over again to food shoppers, so not much is gained. And because the red and green colors don't work well for many color-blind people, they're not a universal solution (real traffic lights use position as well as color as part of their signal).

Adding color when it is not needed creates confusion.

Color coding works best when you are sure people will spend a long time learning and reusing your design, or when you're using a code your audience has already learned.

You'll have to eat a lot of sushi to learn the color code by heart.

Salmon &
Tobiko Tartare
Salmon, yuzu tobiko and
salmon trout roe tartare
with a coriander dressing

Seared Filet or
Hamachi with...

Desire paths

The next time you're in a park or a stretch of grass that's visited by a lot of people, keep an eye out for two things. First, look for the footpaths that a planner or architect has laid down through the park. These paths probably show how a designer, from an aerial view, thought people should move through the space—often in straight lines or a tidy, geometric pattern. Then look for the tracks that people have made as they wander across the grass. These well-worn "desire paths" are often quite different from the paved routes.

Looking down on his plans, the architect thought he'd designed the perfect layout. But when you walk through the park, you can see exactly why people have created the desire paths—taking a shortcut to a gate, avoiding a poorly lit corner, linking up two parallel routes. Walking the desire paths always feels simpler than sticking to the "proper" footpaths.

If you're plotting the user's path through your software, it's important not to fall in love with the neat lines and tidy organization you see in your plans.

Walk through the software repeatedly, and see what catches your eye (squint at your screen layouts!). Watch other people doing the same thing.

Simple organization is about what feels good as you're using the software, not what looks logical in a plan.

People won't always
follow the path you set.

Part 6

Hide

Hide

Hiding features behind a hatch or sliding panel is a popular solution to the problem of simplifying a DVD remote. I own several remote controls that take this approach.

Another way to hide buttons is to use a touch-screen remote control. In those designs, the most frequently used features are on display and the rarely used ones are hidden in menus deeper within the device.

You can buy those kinds of programmable touch-screen remote controls—they're sold on ease of use and they cost about twice as much as a typical DVD player. That shows just how far some people are prepared to go for simplicity.

Whether you go down the expensive high-tech route or add a couple of cents to the cost of your remote control by hiding features behind a plastic hatch, hiding has a big advantage over organizing: users aren't distracted by unwanted details.

For some people, hiding is a first step to removing an unloved feature: hide it, let it wither in the dark, then kill it. I'm dubious of that approach. Terminating any feature means you'll need to go through the arguments I discussed in the *Remove* section, whether or not you've hidden it first. It's usually better to end it quickly.

Hiding anything means putting a barrier between the user and the feature, whether it's a plastic door on a remote control or a sequence of clicks on a website. You must carefully choose what to hide so as not to inconvenience the user.

Hiding some features is a low-cost solution. But which features should you hide?

Infrequent but necessary

Features that mainstreamers rarely use, but which they may need to update, are usually good choices to hide. These features are unlikely to appear in the story you wrote in the *Setting a Vision* section as they're not related to the users' goals so much as who they are or where they are:

- Account details (for instance, setting up your server details or your signature in a desktop email application).

- Options and preferences (such as changing the units in a drawing application from inches to centimeters).

- Location-specific information (such as time and date, though frequently these can be updated automatically).

Failing to include these kinds of controls in your website or application would often make it too general to suit the users' needs.

You'll see settings controls tucked away at the edges of software, away from the important stuff that tends to live at the top or the center of the screen. They are best located on opening pages or on all pages (it's impossible to know when users will want to change these settings, so hide them at the start of a website or at the edge of an application).

When you're looking for features to hide, settings are always a good choice. They are different from infrequently used tasks largely because tasks are focused on an external goal (such as sending a message to a friend) whereas settings are focused on using the software well (such as automatically formatting bullet lists).

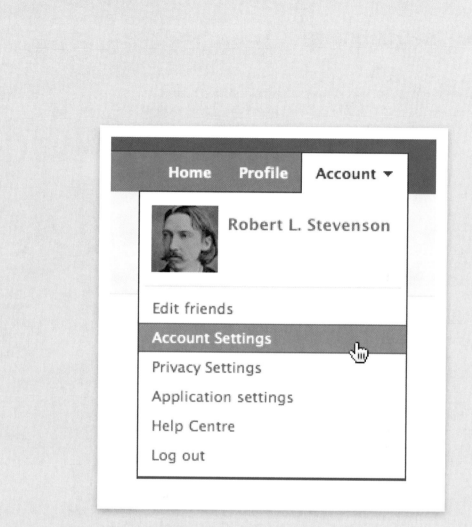

Profile settings that change infrequently are good choices to hide.

Customizing

One approach that I'm not keen on is to let users customize the interface by hiding features according to their needs. To me, this smacks of laziness and indecision on the part of the designers.

It sounds fair and generous to give the user a choice. The trouble is that customizing can be time-consuming and cumbersome. You can customize the myriad floating palettes and toolbars in Microsoft Word should you have the time. But it's a laborious process that requires an understanding of what makes a good user interface. The irony is, you need to learn the vast range of features on offer before you can simplify them.

Even simple interfaces can be painful to customize. My TV receiver lets me shuffle and hide the channels I see on the program guide. This is useful, as the default order seems to be completely random. However, doing this for sixty channels takes hundreds of clicks on the remote control. It's mind-numbingly boring.

Mainstreamers do customize their devices. But they're more interested in personalizing—changing their computer desktop to a picture of their dog—than in redesigning the user interface.

Customizing is more practical when the tools for customizing are simple and when people are adding a few items, rather than rearranging many.

iGoogle and Facebook are good examples of this. However, one of the goals of Facebook is self-expression. Choosing what content to put on your profile is part of the task. So it doesn't seem like a chore.

Customizing can also work when the user is gradually making small changes, such as adding apps and shuffling icons on a smartphone. Even then users often complain that things get out of control as time goes by and they add too much stuff.

In general, users shouldn't have to customize their software. The goal of a word processor is writing. Sifting through features and deciding which ones to show and hide is for experts.

Allowing users to customize their user interface assumes that they will be able to create effective, efficient layouts.

Users can customize
all these buttons in
Microsoft Word. But
is that how they want
to spend their time?

Automatic customization

Some programs try to show and hide features automatically depending on the users' behavior.

The "adaptive menus" in Microsoft Office 2000 show how rocky that road can be.

The idea was that the top-level menus would display only a subset of commonly used commands. If you left your pointer over a menu for a few seconds, or if you clicked on a chevron at the bottom of a menu, it would expand to show you the full set of commands.

As you used the menus, they would remember which commands you used most frequently and adapt so that your favorite commands were visible and the others were hidden.

I recall that a few days or hours after someone had installed Office 2000, he would start walking from desk to desk asking how to turn off this feature (it wasn't easy). Microsoft dropped the idea a few years later. The BBC abandoned a similar attempt to auto-customize its home page.

Instead of making an interface simpler, automatic customization can make it more complex and frustrating to use for three reasons:

- It's hard to get the default menus right. Although most people only use a fraction of the functionality of a large application like Microsoft Word, the features they use vary widely. So what's right for one person is wrong for most others.

- Short menus make users look twice for each feature—first on the short menu, and then again on the long menu. A delay or an extra click to bring up the long menu increases users' irritation.

- Users can't learn where to find items because their position keeps changing.

Unless the algorithm you're using is perfect (and nothing is perfect), it will be wrong often enough to undermine users' confidence and make your interface feel complex and confusing.

Imagine what it would be like if someone rearranged your closets every night while you were asleep. That's how annoying automatic customization can be.

Default

Tools

✓ABC	Spelling and Grammar...	F7
	Word Count...	
	Look Up Reference...	
	Online Collaboration	▶
📧	Envelopes and Labels...	
	Customize...	
	Options...	
	⌄	

Expand

Expanded

Tools

✓ABC	Spelling and Grammar...	F7
	Language	▶
	Word Count...	
📄	AutoSummarize...	
	AutoCorrect...	
	Look Up Reference...	
	Track Changes	▶
	Merge Documents...	
	Protect Document...	
	Online Collaboration	▶
	Mail Merge...	
📧	Envelopes and Labels...	
	Letter Wizard...	
	Macro	▶
	Templates and Add-Ins...	
	Customize...	
	Options...	

Progressive disclosure

Often a feature has a few core controls for mainstreamers and extended, precision controls for experts. Hiding the precision controls is a good way to keep things simple.

The Save dialog box is a classic example of this. The basic feature is nothing more than two core questions:

- what would you like to call this file?

- where, from a list of options, would you like to save it?

But experts want something richer: extended options to create a new folder for the document, to search your hard disk for places to save the document, to browse your hard disk in other ways, and to save the file in a special format.

Rather than show everything, the Save dialog box opens with the mainstream version but lets users expand it to see the expert version.

The box remembers which version you prefer and uses that in the future. This is better than automatic customization because it's the user who chooses how the interface should look.

This is also better than regular customizing because the user makes the choices as she goes, rather than having a separate task of creating the menu. This means mainstreamers aren't forced to customize.

That model, of core features and extended features, is a classic way to provide simplicity as well as power. For instance, mainstream computer users know to left-click on interfaces to make something happen. Experts know that right-clicking will bring up a menu of additional options.

Google's Advanced Search features include keyword search, in-site search, Boolean search, language-restricted search, region-specific search, linked pages, file-type restricted search, date constraints, copyright constraints, prioritization of keywords, "safe" search, and comparison search. Of these, only keyword search is visible on the main interface; the others are hidden. User testing will tell you if you're getting it right or not.

Set users' expectations with clear cues in the right context.

Untitled 3 (Word Processing)

View Full Screen Outline   Sections Text Box Shapes Table Charts Comment   iWork.com   Inspector Media Colors Fonts

Save As: Untitled 3.pages

Macintosh HD

▶ DEVICES
▶ SHARED
▶ PLACES
▶ SEARCH FOR

Applications
Desktop
Library
System
Users
Voumes

Hello

☑ Include preview in document
☐ Save copy as: Word Document
▼ Advanced Options:
   ☑ Copy audio and movies into document
   ☐ Copy template images into document

☐ Hide extension   New Folder   Cancel   Save

Untitled 3 (Word Processing)

View Full Screen Outline   Sections Text Box Shapes Table Charts Comment   iWork.com   Inspector Media Colors Fonts

Helvetica

0   100   500

Save As: Untitled 3.pages   ▼

Where: Macintosh HD

Hello world

                           Cancel   Save

Staged disclosure

One alternative to hiding features in another part of your software is to reveal features as the user progresses deeper into the interface.

This approach works well when all users naturally seek more complexity as they progress. For instance, a user might start searching using a simple text box and then see filtering and sorting options on the results screen.

Staged disclosure is often required for processes such as booking forms, but there are rules.

- Set the scene. When we tested one online checkout process, users found the transition from shopping cart to checkout disorienting. When the same process started with the words "Welcome to secure checkout," their problems vanished.

- Tell a story. Users expect the sequence to unfold like a story, find out what that story is, and follow it. One online order form I tested started by asking users to enter their name and address. The owner explained that if there was a problem at a later stage, the company would still be able to contact the customer. But customers hated it. When the sequence followed a simple story ("What do you want? Now where should I send it?"), the conversion rate increased.

- Speak the users' language. Processes tend to exist because the user has to conform to a bureaucratic process (like a passport application) or a technical procedure (like setting up a modem) and bureaucracy and technology breed jargon. For insiders, jargon is compact and specific. For novices, one unfamiliar word of jargon is more complex than an entire familiar sentence.

- Reveal information in bite-sized chunks. If the chunks are too big, users feel the form is too complex. If the form is divided into lots of tiny nibbles, users feel the form is inefficient and tedious. Each chunk should be complete and self-contained (for instance, don't divide the address across two screens).

Wizards are a form of staged disclosure, but they often break all these rules: they fail to tell a story, they use jargon without explanation, fail to explain consequences, fail to set the scene, and use chunks that are too big or too small.

Staged disclosure works best when the steps in the process meet users' expectations.

If you get it wrong, users feel like they're being pushed down a chute.

X doesn't mark the spot

Not long ago, I was reading the *New York Times* online and I came across this passage:

> This is a week of suspended animation in the city, in between holidays, when the great systems of New York—the schools, the courts, the communications media, Wall Street, City Hall, the bodegas in Queens—slow to an administrative crawl or shut down altogether.

Being English, my first response to this was, "What's a bodega?" So I did what I normally do when I don't know a word: I highlighted it so I could copy and paste it into Google. Something surprising happened: a little question mark icon appeared next to my highlight. I clicked on it and up popped a window with a definition of the word (bodega: A small grocery store, sometimes combined with a wineshop, in certain Hispanic communities). The same thing works for every single word in the article; it doesn't matter if you click on "media", "animation", "the", or "a"; there's a definition for every word.

What's clever about this is that the feature is hidden, but it reveals itself precisely when you need it.

It takes courage to hide things as completely as this. The design team must have worried that users would never find their work: "We've gone to all this trouble, we should *show* people this feature."

The thing is, overemphasizing hidden features can lead to a mess. Think what would have happened if the *New York Times* had not hidden the dictionary so well.

If they had put hyperlinks in the text, they would have distracted and irritated readers. If they had put hyperlinks on every word, the page would have been a complete mess. If they had picked out a few words, they would have faced the expensive task of editing every article to decide which words were worth defining. By trying to show off the feature, they would have been dragged into a messy, ugly, expensive quagmire.

Sadly, most attempts to hide features are like this. It's like hiding buttons on the DVD remote control behind a glass door.

The *New York Times'* solution illustrates what you must do to hide successfully. First, hide something as completely as possible. Second, make features reveal themselves just when they're needed.

This is a week of suspended animation in the city, in between holidays, when the great systems of New York — the schools, the courts, the communications m ? a, Wall Street, City Hall, the bodegas in Queens — slow to an administrative crawl or shut down altogether.

The *New York Times'* dictionary feature is hidden until you highlight a word.

Cues and clues

Choosing a label for hidden features can seem tricky. How do you explain the complex and subtle extras that have been hidden?

Often you'll find extras hiding behind a vague label like "more" or a patronizing one like Google's Advanced Search. Although this is a common solution, it's not ideal. One of the reasons for hiding complexity is to prevent the user from feeling stupid. Labeling a button "advanced" effectively tells the user that she's not qualified to go there. That's not a feel-good moment.

An alternative is to use a label that will only appeal to a certain group. If you look at most computer manufacturers' websites, you'll see they swamp customers with technical details. I've watched mainstreamers lose confidence as they read about L2 cache and motherboard speed options, but to experts this is essential information.

Apple's website presents its products in a breezy, magazine style that suits mainstreamers. But in one corner is the label Tech Specs. Mainstreamers stick to the pictures and headlines. But for customers who really want to know about graphics processors, this link pops off the page. It's a phrase that they're attuned to, but that mainstreamers aren't interested in.

Adobe Illustrator has a more subtle solution. Some of the drawing tools have advanced features that are indicated by a small arrow on the tool palette. You click once to select the basic tool, or click and hold to see the advanced options.

What's nice about this approach is that it is an invitation to explore, rather than a label that attempts to explain what comes next. It's also specific: the context sets the expectation that the additional functionality has something to do with the nearby tool. Experts are happy to follow those invitations because they like to explore and learn. Mainstreamers are happy to put off exploring until they have gained confidence or until they need to. No one is labeled as inadequate.

Interfaces that hide well are elegant: they use the most subtle cue possible to suggest the location and nature of the additional functionality.

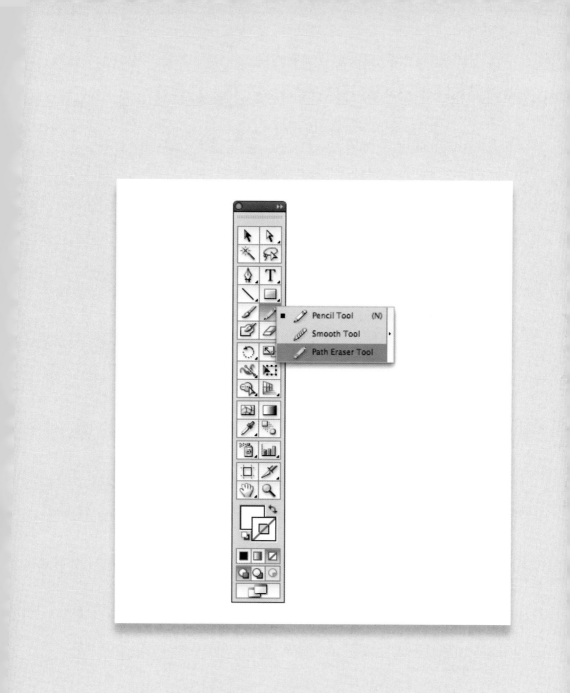

**Small cues can hint
at hidden features.**

Making things easy to find

Where you place a label is more important than how big it is.

Keith Lang, who designed the interface for Skitch and Comic Life, an award-winning drawing application, points to two examples from his own work. "We gave Skitch advanced features you could get by holding down a key on your computer," he says. "We wanted to reveal these features, so we put a pop-up help box at the top of the screen whenever you used the toolbar, but most users don't see it even though it's pretty big. On Comic Life we used a small label on one of the tool palettes to explain how to use it, and that works well."

The difference is down to what Jef Raskin (one of the original creators of the Macintosh) calls the users' *locus of attention*—the area of the screen that the user is concentrating on.

When a user first looks at a screen or begins a new task, her locus of attention is wide. If you watch eye-tracking studies you will see users scanning all over a screen when they encounter a new website. As the user concentrates on a task, her locus of attention narrows. In eye-tracking studies, you'll see users focus in on one or two areas of the screen or start reading along a body of text after they've made their initial assessment. When users have a problem, they tend to concentrate even more on the problem area of the screen. (In *The Humane Interface*, Raskin cites this as the reason that users often can't find help when they need it: they're too busy concentrating on the area of the screen where they're having a problem.)

What Keith Lang found with Skitch was that the large label placed far away from the locus of attention was ineffective. In Comic Life he found a small label placed within the locus of attention worked well.

In the *New York Times* example, the question mark icon appeared directly over the word that I'd selected, in the center of my locus of attention. Even though the hidden feature was revealed unexpectedly, it was unmissable.

Make sure your users will encounter a clue on their journey. But don't block their path.

After you hide

Hiding, then, depends on four things:

- Hide one-time settings and options.

- Hide precision controls, but let expert users choose to keep them revealed.

- Don't force or expect mainstreamers to customize, but offer this option for experts.

- Hide elegantly; that is, hide completely and reveal just in time.

The three strategies so far—remove, organize, and hide—fit together neatly: remove what you don't need, organize what you do, hide what you can. But the final strategy, displace, is really about rethinking the interface entirely.

Hiding works, as long as no one has to seek too long.

Part 7

Displace

Displace

The fourth strategy for simplifying the DVD remote control is to cheat.

Designers who take this approach strip the remote control down to a few basic actions, like play and pause, and manage all the other features via a menu on the TV screen. The remote control itself is approachable, easy to understand, and simple to use.

Another advantage of this strategy is that it makes good use of the remote control. Users only have a few buttons to learn and they can easily be distinguished by touch—so it's easy to use in the dark while you're watching a DVD.

It's also far cheaper to make use of the existing TV screen than to add an expensive display to the remote control. The TV screen is well suited to this. It can display an infinite number of different menus and it's bound to be in a location where the user can see it clearly.

The disadvantage of this approach is that if you displace all the features, then it's hard to guess what the remote control can do. If you had to find and access the play function by navigating into a menu, that might seem obscure and tedious. That's why most people end up leaving a few basic controls on the remote.

Also, though you've simplified the remote control, you still have the problem of designing a simple on-screen menu system (using the strategies of remove, organize, and hide).

But if you understand the trade-offs, displacing the right roles to the right devices works well. One of the secrets of creating simple experiences is putting the right functionality on the right platform or part of the system.

Why not take some buttons off the remote and use an on-screen menu instead?

Displacing between devices

What's easy on one platform can feel complex on another.

RunKeeper is an iPhone app and website that lets users track their exercise routines. On the iPhone, recording a run is as simple as pressing start on the app and slipping the phone in your pocket. As you run, the phone monitors your location using GPS. At the end of the run, you hit stop and the app saves the date, time, and duration of your run, a map of where you went, the total distance, the split time for each mile run, the profile of the hills you covered, and an estimate of the calories you burned. Capturing that data is as easy as pressing a button.

On the other hand, the mobile app can't display all the information about your run on the phone's small screen.

If you want to enter data on the website, you can enter most (but not all) of the above using an online form. It's a slow process of drawing a path on a map and filling in numerous fields.

When it comes to reviewing your data, the mobile app doesn't display all the information about your run on the phone, just a brief summary. The website, designed to be viewed on a large computer screen, has enough space to comfortably display far more data. It's easier to review the detailed results sitting at your desk using a big screen.

RunKeeper takes advantage of the strengths of each platform. The task of gathering information on split times is simplest on the mobile phone, so that's where it goes. But you can only view those times on the website, where there's enough space to display them. The result is that the overall experience feels simple.

**The RunKeeper mobile
app is best for recording
data; the website is
best for reading it.**

Mobile vs. desktop

Some of the limitations of mobile devices will change as technology gradually improves. But devices will always have strengths and weaknesses. Sometimes it makes sense to displace some parts of a task, like entering data, onto a different platform.

Mobile	Desktop/laptop
Photograph anything	Photograph the user (via a webcam)
Input small amounts of text	Input large amounts of text
Slow to moderate data speeds	Moderate to fast data speeds
Display small amounts of information	Display large amounts of information
Store moderate amounts of data	Store very large amounts of data
Used anywhere	Used when seated
Aware of precise location and orientation	Some awareness of location
Connected to other devices via wireless networks	Connected directly to other devices via cables and wireless networks

Today's mobile devices are great for recording what users see and hear, and where they go. But entering large amounts of text is uncomfortable.

Displacing to the user

About ten years ago, I was asked to design a travel planner for a tourism website. Planning a holiday is complex. Travelers have a limited amount of time, but they're often able to stretch things a little; they have a limited budget, but again it will change; they are in a specific location, but they're prepared to move around; they have specific interests, but they're often looking for novel experiences. In other words, everything is up for grabs.

I decided that traveling was about managing time and space, so I began my smart travel planner with a map. I invited users to inspect locations on the map, like the Edinburgh Castle or the Science Museum in London. Users would be able to see how long they should allow for each location. They would then add the location to an itinerary where they could rearrange the items. The smart travel planner would allow for journey times, meals, and accommodations. This meant they'd be able to see what they could fit into each day and they would be alerted if they had tried to cram in too much.

When I tried it out, users hated it. Even though I'd designed an open-ended task, they felt that they were too constrained and that the smart travel planner was continually judging their plans. It never got built.

A few years later, I was lucky enough to be asked to try again. I chose a stripped-down approach. I let users create folders, name them as they pleased, and put whatever they wanted into the folders.

Users came up with labels I'd expected (days of the week, locations) and ones I didn't expect ("under £10," "rainy days"), but which made perfect sense.

It was exciting to watch users set their own success criteria. Each user did as much planning as suited her. Some users created precise travel plans, others just created lists of ideas. From the outside, some of the travel plans looked complex, but they always made sense to the users.

The complex part of travel planning is handling the ambiguity. But the simple interface had left this task to the users. I'd displaced the complexity into the users' heads.

My Travel Plan

LOCATION	ACTIVITY	TIME
Bath	Excelsior Hotel	N/A
Bath	The Roman Baths	0930-1130
Bath	Train to Oxford	1042-1153
Oxford	The King's Head	1230-1400
Oxford	Punting	1415-1515
Oxford	Ashmolean Museum	1530-1700
Oxford	Train to London	1722-1835

Not enough time. Remove activities or reduce time allocations

STRATFORD-UPON-AVON

OXFORD

LONDON

BATH

The Roman Baths
A fascinating treasure trove of anicient history with a chance to see the baths themselves, a computer-generated reconstruction and artefacts including a collection of Roman curses.

Mon-Fri 0900-1830 (includes Bank Holidays)
Sat-Sun 0900-1730
Christmas: Closed

£10 Adults, £5 Children / Student / Over 65

Allow 1 hour ▼   Add this

◄ ● ● ○ ○ ○ ►

Tuesday

Kid's things

Travel discounts

What users do best

The reason the basic travel planner felt simple is because it let the users and computers do what they're best at.

Computers are good at storing detailed information accurately. You only have to tell a computer your phone number once and it will remember it forever. People are terrible at remembering those kinds of detail. The basic travel planner gave the task of remembering to the computer.

Computers are good at calculating accurately. But travel planning begins with approximate calculation and imagining how an itinerary might unfold, both of which are better done by people. The basic travel planner left users in charge of making sense of the plans.

People like to be in control of outcomes. The smart travel planner forced users to create one kind of plan. If there were too many tasks, it showed a warning message; too few and it felt incomplete. The basic travel planner left it up to the user to decide when they had done enough planning.

The basic travel planner left users with the tasks of forming a goal and deciding how to organize their notes. These are complex for a computer, but they are tasks that people are good at, so the basic travel planner felt simple to use.

The smart travel planner tried to set a goal and forced users to organize information in a way that didn't always suit, so it felt complex to use.

One of the keys to making an experience feel simple is to understand which tasks to hand over to the computer and which tasks to leave for the user:

People	Computers
Setting goals and planning	Following procedures
Approximate calculation	Accurate calculation
Recognizing information	Storing and retrieving details
Making schematics	Making copies
Choosing from small lists	Sorting large lists
Estimating	Measuring
Imagining	Cross-referencing detailed information

When the user is directing, and the computer guiding, the experience feels simpler.

Creating open experiences

Clever designers often simplify by making one component serve several purposes. For instance, in some cars, the rear windshield heating element is also the radio antenna.

You can reduce complexity in software by designing features that can be used for several purposes. The task of choosing how to use them is displaced to users.

For example, have you noticed how many ways there are to save items on sites like Amazon? You can drop an item in your shopping basket for later, take it out of your shopping basket, and put it in your "saved items," add it to a wish list, or set up lists for weddings and birthdays.

Each of these features has specialized functions, like the ability to publish wish lists to friends. But mostly, they all do the same thing: save an item to buy later.

Users have to learn several features, then remember which one they used to save an item and how to get to it again.

This also requires a lot of effort on the store's part: maintaining code, providing help and technical support, making sure it all works, and finding a place within the website for all these features to live.

When I come across similar features like this, I look to see if they can be combined into a general tool.

Imagine if these lists were all in one place: a set of folders within the shopping basket. You could name the folders (Wedding, Birthday, Travel Books) and choose whether to publish them to a friend. One feature could do the job of four.

It's important to prompt users with ideas for the different ways the feature might be put to use. Suggesting some ideas for naming their lists would be enough to start users thinking about what they could do with the feature.

Simplifying by combining similar features is a neat solution. The result may not be perfectly tailored to each use, but there are significant advantages. It's easier to find one feature than to pick it out from several similar features. It's easier to learn one feature than several. And it's easier to maintain just one feature.

In some cars, the rear window heating element heating element doubles as a radio antenna, simplifying the design.

Kitchen knives and pianos

The ultimate in simple interfaces are ones that make sense to experts and mainstreamers alike.

Take a really simple device like a kitchen knife. A novice can use a kitchen knife to get a "good enough" outcome without much instruction or help. An expert can use the same knife to get "precision control"—chopping quickly, carving shapes, and so on. The knife is the same, but the expert's technique turns it into an expert tool.

The same goes for a piano. A novice can pick out a tune without any training and would probably tell you that it felt pretty simple. An expert can play a sonata without much trouble. The difference is technique.

What makes these experiences feel simple is that the experts and mainstreamers are free to set their own goals. They have their own expectations of how much effort it will take to achieve them, based on their past experience. Playing the piano only feels like a chore when the music is at the limits of one's training.

It's the same with open experiences like the simple travel planner: they often work well for experts and novices. Letting users define success (a complete travel plan or a list of ideas) is important. So is giving them a tool that is simple enough that they can imagine how to achieve their goals.

These interfaces don't always suit the middle ground, who can see what an expert can do, but lack the technique to get there. That explains the appeal of kitchen gadgets for chopping onions and eggs, or electronic pianos that fill in tunes with a backing track.

Those kinds of gadgets offer assistance, but the price is clutter. Imagine a kitchen without a knife, but packed with specialized chopping devices.

The trick with open interfaces is to minimize the number of "handy" gadgets for the middle ground.

A kitchen knife meets
the expectations
and needs of expert
and mainstreamer.

Unstructured data

Filling in forms is an irksome task that frequently feels stilted and complex. One reason for this is that users are being asked to format information so that it makes sense to the software or some distant bureaucracy.

One way of getting around this is to let the user take on the task of making sense of the data. An example of this is Ta-da List, 37signals' basic to-do list website. The creators point out that they intentionally kept data entry simple; for instance, there was no way to add a due date to a task. They figured that if people wanted they could just add "Due 17 January" to the description of the item.

When the user is making sense of his own notes, this approach works just fine. It's simple, open, and "human." Don't assume you need to make users fill in a structured form.

If the data needs to be processed by a computer (for instance, if the tasks need to be sorted into date order) then the data needs to be structured. But often the computer can recognize and structure the data in the users' notes.

Some email software looks for phrases like "next Tuesday" or "1-800-654-3001" in emails and turns them into clickable links that create an appointment in the user's calendar or dial the number on his phone.

The user is free to write emails in loosely structured, human terms. The computer takes on the task of figuring out whether there's any data in there that needs to be structured or acted on.

One of my pet hates is online forms that require me to enter my credit card details without spaces or that tell me off for using brackets in phone numbers. It's easy to write software that can deal with this—it's lazy and rude for companies to force customers to stick rigidly to their data entry rules.

Let the computer take on some of the responsibility for structuring the data and you'll simplify the user experience.

Apple's "data detectors" look for addresses in emails and let you add them to your contact database.

Trust

Displacing tasks is easiest when you're dividing them between two devices that have to be used together in a specific way. The DVD remote control has to be used with the TV display, so it's fairly easy to see what each should do.

When you're not sure how the devices will be used together, displacing becomes harder.

You can't be sure how the RunKeeper mobile app and website will be used. Some people may not have mobile phones and will just want to use the website. Some people may stick exclusively to using their mobile phone. Some people may do a bit of both.

When that uncertainty creeps in, you find yourself duplicating functionality between platforms. So it is with RunKeeper, where only a little of the functionality is displaced between website and mobile.

You need a sense of certainty to be able to displace tasks effectively.

If you're going to displace tasks to be the responsibility of the user, you have to trust that the user will take on those tasks.

Trusting the audience is hard. Designers are used to watching them fail in user tests. Programmers are used to thinking of all the ways a system could go wrong so that they can design for error. Product managers want to provide users with interactive tools that take on all the hard work. And sometimes the unspoken purpose of software is to make users behave in ways that are convenient for the designer.

In other words, we often treat users like children. But in protecting users from making errors or finding their own solutions, we often deny them the chance to make their own decisions. No wonder users often feel rebellious or resentful toward computers.

The only way to build that trust is to try out prototypes and mock-ups with users. When you get the balance of tasks right, letting users focus on choosing and directing, and having the computer focus on remembering and calculating, you'll create experiences that are simple and surprising because of the creativity users can bring to them.

Computers often make users uncomfortable because they control and direct users' behavior. Simple experiences require trust.

Part 8

Before we go

Conservation of complexity

Making things simple can sometimes feel like a game of Whac-A-Mole. Bash one complexity on the head and another pops up elsewhere.

Take the example of the online bank statement in Section 4: Remove. The original design had the user choose a month and a year, then asked the bank for the corresponding statement. This was straightforward to program but felt harder to use thanks, in part, to the high risk of errors.

In the revised design the user picked from a list of available statements. This felt simple to use and eliminated errors, but was more complex to program and put more load on the bank's server as it checked which statements were available.

While he was part of the team developing the Macintosh, Larry Tesler summarized this in his Law of Conservation of Complexity:

> Every application must have an inherent amount of irreducible complexity. The only question is: who will have to deal with it?

Designing simple user experiences often turns out not to be about "How can I make this simpler?" but rather "Where should I move the complexity?"

- Should a task be automated (like autofocus on the Flip) or controlled by the user (like tapping the screen to focus the camera on the iPhone)?

- Should an interface have many specific controls (like a hi-fi) or a few general controls (like an iPod)?

- Should a task be completed at one time (like signing up for Facebook) or spread over time (like customizing a Tumblr blog)?

- Should a task be handled by the conscious mind (like using on-screen controls to filter search results) or the unconscious brain (like focusing on the green District line on the London Underground map)?

The secret to creating a simple user experience is to shift complexity into the right place, so that each moment feels simple.

Bash away—but complexity will keep popping up.

Details

The last time I visited Paris, I loaded an app onto my mobile phone to help me navigate the Metro. I typed in the start and finish of my journey and the app calculated the best route, telling me which lines to use, which connections to make, and how long it would take. It seemed perfect until I descended into the subway. Then I realized I was missing one piece of information.

The app didn't tell me which direction the trains would be going, which, in the Paris Metro, is indicated by the station at the end of the line. I found myself standing in a busy tunnel as people pushed by while I scrolled around the tiny on-screen version of the Metro map trying to locate the end station for the first leg of my journey. Simplicity often depends on details.

Missing details can have a catastrophic effect or cause irritation that builds over time. When you're fixing small details, the question that often comes up is: why bother? Is it really worth spending half a day fixing these drop-down menus to save a customer a few seconds?

For mass-market software, it's never just one customer: it's thousands, sometimes millions of customers using the software repeatedly. The few seconds of customer time quickly adds up to years. A tiny frustration becomes a frequent annoyance. Finding an extra half-day to devise a solution is a small problem compared to creating an army of irritated customers.

Take Line 9—
but which direction?

Simplicity happens in the user's head

If you overload any machine, it starts to creak and slow down under the stress. The same is true for people. Give us too many things to remember and we'll forget, too many tasks to juggle and we'll drop one, too many decisions to make and we'll freeze.

Making software *usable* means not exceeding your users' capacity. However, users always demand more detailed information, more choices, more stuff—it's human nature. So the tendency is to design usable experiences right up to that maximum—stopping just short of overloading the user.

Simple experiences don't do that. They leave the user with plenty to spare. What happens to all that "unused" capacity?

A travel firm once asked my company to compare customers' experiences of researching holidays online and through brochures. Watching customers plough through websites, reviewing detailed information and options, we were struck by how tense and irritable they were.

The brochures were far simpler: some large photos of a resort, a few icons highlighting key features, and a table of prices. When they looked through the brochures, customers were relaxed, imagining what the holiday could be like. They enjoyed themselves.

Simple experiences leave users with enough capacity to think about how what they're doing fits in with their lives.

A simple camera like The Flip lets users concentrate on capturing the moment, a simple DVD remote control allows users to focus on the movie.

Don't try to fill the user's mind with your design. Designing for simplicity leaves your user enough room to fill in details from his or her life and create a richer, more meaningful experience.

Give your users enough space to use their imagination.

Photo Credits

Part 4

Remove

Page 67, Photo courtesy iStockphoto, © Grigory Bibikov, Image 10362465

Page 69, Photo Copyright Virgin Media

Page 71, Photo courtesy iStockphoto, © Jami Garrison, Image 2252631

Page 73, Photo courtesy iStockphoto, © MBPHOTO, INC., Image 918432

Page 79, Photo courtesy iStockphoto, © Mark Wragg, Image 13558859

Page 81, Photo courtesy iStockphoto, © tolgakolcak, Image 7265127

Page 83, Photo courtesy iStockphoto, © Peter Garbet, Image 5742149

Page 87, Photo courtesy iStockphoto, © Conrad Lottenbach, Image 3131848

Page 101, Photo courtesy iStockphoto, © mphotoi, Image 3431237

Page 103, Photo thanks to DDB UK; Illustrator: Pete Mould

Page 105, Photo: Ray Yuen

Page 109, Photo courtesy iStockphoto, © malerapaso, Image 12566021 (picture frame)

Page 109, Photo courtesy iStockphoto, © wsfurlan, Image 8528913 (mobile phone)

Part 5

Organize

Page 115, Photo courtesy iStockphoto, © PLAINVIEW, Image 13334346

Page 123, Photo courtesy iStockphoto, © Luis Santana, Image 2329511

Page 125, Photo courtesy iStockphoto, © Thomas Arbour, Image 12878280

Page 129, Photo courtesy iStockphoto, © Anna Yu, Image 8162485 (basketball)

Page 129, Photo courtesy iStockphoto, © Matteo Rinaldi, Image 12117545 (golf ball)

Page 129, Photo courtesy iStockphoto, © Tomasz Pietryszek, Image 12133382 (tennis ball)

Page 129, Photo courtesy iStockphoto, © Chris Scredon, Image 7337356 (soccer ball)

Page 131, Photo: Copyright Transport for London

Page 133, Photo: Copyright Adam Wilson

Page 135, Photo thanks to Andrew Skudder

Part 6

Hide

Page 149, Photo courtesy iStockphoto, © James Pauls, Image 3098674

Page 155, Photo courtesy iStockphoto, © Steve Harmon, Image 1035401

Page 157, Photo courtesy iStockphoto, © Alina555, Image 4716967

Part 7

Displace

Page 165, Photo courtesy iStockphoto, © Matt Jeacock, Image 9316437

Page 169, Photo courtesy iStockphoto, © Neustockimages, Image 7418248

Page 171, Photo courtesy Honda PR

Page 173, Photo courtesy iStockphoto, © Matt Jeacock, Image 13726223

Page 177, Photo courtesy iStockphoto, © René Mansi, Image 184532

Part 8

Before we go

Page 181, Photo © Ricky Leong

Page 185, Photo courtesy iStockphoto, © Matt Jeacock, Image 12394740

Index

your world. our stock.

suit
business
umbrella

teamwork coworkers men

DJ
music
glamor

shopping
casual
woman

businesswoman portrait nature

Get 20% off
any purchase over $50 USD

www.istockphoto.com/simpleanduseable

iStockphoto®